The Message of Mark

Morna D. Hooker

The Message of Mark

EPWORTH PRESS London

First published 1983
by Epworth Press

All enquiries should be addressed to
The Epworth Press
Room 195
1 Central Buildings
Westminster
London SW1H 9NR

7162 0390 1

Typeset by Gloucester Typesetting Services
and printed in Great Britain by
Clifford Frost Ltd, Wimbledon

Contents

Preface

The origins of this book lie in two courses of lectures on 'The Christology of Mark', given in Oxford to the Vacation Term for Biblical Study, the first in 1964, and the second in 1981. The lectures have subsequently been adapted for use in addressing various audiences. Two of the earlier lectures have now been rewritten, in order to make this collection less repetitive and more of a unity, but otherwise they have been left more or less as delivered. I am grateful to those who have heard me speak on this subject and who, by their response, have encouraged me to publish these lectures.

M.D.H.

ONE

'The Beginning of the Gospel . . .'

When one of my colleagues learned that I was planning to give a series of lectures on the christology of Mark, he exclaimed in great astonishment: 'How can anyone possibly give a whole series on that subject? What will you say after the first quarter of an hour?' His comment is typical of the way in which Mark is commonly regarded. In spite of the fact that his Gospel has been as it were rehabilitated in the last hundred years, one has the feeling that his chief and perhaps only claim to merit is that he was probably the first evangelist. If I had chosen the christology of John as my subject, that would have occasioned no surprise, for he has long been regarded as one of the two great theologians of the early church. The other two evangelists, Matthew and Luke, also have some claim to be treated as theologians. But what are we to say of Mark?

For centuries, Mark was the Cinderella among the Synoptic Gospels. On the authority of Augustine, it was believed that Mark had copied and abbreviated Matthew – and why should one bother with an abbreviation, when one has the full account? So Mark was neglected, as an inferior Gospel, written, not by an apostle, but by the companion of an apostle. The wonder is that somehow it crept into the canon, and was not discarded as unnecessary. Then, in the nineteenth century, scholars realized that in fact the boot was on the other foot. It was not Mark who had copied and abbreviated Matthew, but Matthew who had copied and expanded Mark. The belief that Mark was the earliest of the Gospels meant that scholars treated it with a new respect; for if this was the earliest Gospel, then it was the closest to the events which it described, and must surely be the most reliable. Nineteenth-century New Testament scholarship was dominated by the quest for the historical Jesus – the desire to discover Jesus as he really was, not as the church had interpreted him – and in that quest Mark took on a new importance. According to one ancient tradition, Mark had recorded the memoirs of Peter, and that suggested that his material was reliable.[1] Accordingly, Mark was hailed as a historian and a biographer by the nineteenth-century liberal theologians. His restoration to favour made a lasting impression on New Testament scholarship – and an even more lasting impression on popular understanding of Jesus. For years, most 'Lives of Jesus' were based on the outline of the ministry given by Mark.[2] Above all, the dramatic turning-point at Caesarea Philippi – the famous so-called watershed of the Gospel – has impressed itself on Mark's readers. Because *he* saw the ministry of Jesus this way, thousands of Christians have seen it that way too.

But then came the reaction. The work of form critics such as Dibelius and Bultmann pointed to the fact that the material in the Gospels had not, originally, been part of a connected narrative, but consisted of individual, isolated stories about Jesus. The stories about Jesus had been told and retold by early Christian preachers and teachers, and Mark had gathered these stories together and retold them in his turn, putting them together in a haphazard order, 'like pearls on a string'. Back in the second century, Papias had said that Mark had not written 'in order', by which he presumably meant chronological order. The work of the form critics supported this judgment. But this meant that Mark's Gospel could no longer be used as the basis of a life of Jesus. Mark was no longer regarded as the biographer of Jesus, but as an editor. In scholarly circles, his Gospel (taken as a literary unity) once again went into decline; now, attention was concentrated on the individual units that made up the

Gospels, and the information that they could provide about the faith of the early Christian community which had preserved them.

It will not, I hope, be regarded as a sexist remark if I suggest that only a man could have used the phrase 'like pearls on a string' to suggest a haphazard arrangement of material. Any woman would have spotted at once the flaw in the analogy: pearls need to be carefully selected and graded. And gradually it has dawned on New Testament scholars that this is precisely what the evangelists have done with their material. Their arrangements are anything but haphazard. The stories may not be in order chronologically – but they most certainly have an order. And if the order of material in one Gospel differs from that in another, this is not because the evangelists disagreed about chronology, but because each of them, by his arrangement of the material, was trying to make a particular theological point. And so it is that with the rise of redaction criticism, which concentrates on the question 'What was each evangelist trying to do?', Mark has come back into favour. For if, as still seems most probable, his Gospel was the first of the four to be written, then the question of what he was aiming to do when he set out the good news about Jesus in this new way is of particular interest.

This very brief account of the different ways in which scholars have approached the Gospels during the past hundred years or so will, I hope, demonstrate why attitudes to Mark have changed so much. What one finds in the Gospels depends very much on what one looks for; how one views Mark depends very much on the questions one asks. Earlier generations tended to treat the evangelists as straightforward recorders of events, and the questions they asked were primarily historical. Reading Mark, they asked questions about what Jesus had said and done – even about what he had thought. With the rise of form criticism, the questions changed; now scholars were concerned with what the early church believed about Jesus, and why the first Christians had valued these particular stories. Today, we may well feel that we still want to ask both these sets of questions. But we can only do so (with any hope of success!) after we have begun with what we have – with Mark's account. Our first questions must be about him: What was *he* trying to do? What was it that *he* believed? And why did *he* write the particular things that he did?

Most of us, when we pick up a book in a library or bookshop, will look at the opening page, to see what it is about. If we look at the opening page of Mark, we may hope to discover what this particular book is about. But the first thing we realize is that this page is somewhat different in character from the rest of the book: things happen here that happen nowhere else. The very first verse seems to be a kind of title to the book. Mark plans to tell us the gospel – that is, the good news – about Jesus, who is the Messiah and the Son of God. Then comes an opening paragraph about John the Baptist. But wait a moment! What is John the Baptist doing here? We are so used to the story that we do not realize the oddity of its opening lines. The beginning of the good news about Jesus is not a story about Jesus himself but about John. Let us try to see what Mark is doing. He introduces John with a quotation from the Old Testament – or rather, with two quotations. This is the only occasion in the Gospel where Mark himself (as distinct from the characters in the story) appeals to the Old Testament, and he manages to get his reference wrong! The words he quotes come from Isaiah and Malachi, and from them we learn that John is sent to prepare the way of the Lord. This means that if John has completed his task, the next to arrive on the scene must be the Lord. And the person who comes next is, of course, Jesus; with his arrival we read about the rending of the heavens, the descent of the Holy Spirit, the voice from heaven, and the battle between Jesus and Satan in the wilderness.

The important fact to notice in these opening verses of Mark is that the events described here are different in character from what takes place in most of the remaining pages of the Gospel. Elsewhere, though unusual things happen, we do not find visions or voices from heaven (except once, in chapter 9); nor do we read about the activity of the Holy Spirit and Satan (apart from a discussion about them in chapter 3); we do not even have the meaning of what is going on spelt out for us by Mark with the help of Old Testament texts. In other words, we have here a concentration of christological material – information about the identity of Jesus and the meaning of his ministry. Remarkably, it is concentrated into these few verses, before the ministry of Jesus begins. Several times over, Mark spells out, clearly and openly, who Jesus is.

A glance at the New English Bible will show that the translators responsible for that version regarded the first thirteen verses of the Gospel as forming a distinct section within it. The belief that a division should be made at this point, after v. 13, goes back to a suggestion of R. H. Lightfoot, who argued that the printed Greek texts of his day were wrong to leave a gap after the end of v. 8, and that the gap should be moved to the end of v. 13.[3] A small gap in a page of Greek text might seem a minor alteration, of little importance – at least as far as exegesis of the Gospel is concerned. In fact, Lightfoot's insight into Mark's structure has been of great importance, and has influenced almost all subsequent commentators. For his suggestion sprang from the realization that in these first thirteen verses Mark gives us, not two or three incidents leading up to the ministry of Jesus which put his activity into context, but a christological section which provides the key to understanding the rest of the Gospel.[4] In this introductory section he reveals to us the secret of Jesus' identity, so that in the pages that follow we may appreciate the significance of events which are misunderstood by almost all the characters in the drama. Later we shall look at the theme of the so-called messianic secret which dominates much of the rest of the Gospel. At this stage, however, we may well be inclined to ask 'What secret?' On Mark's opening page there is no secret, for the truth about Jesus is blurted out several times over. And that means that reading the rest of the Gospel is rather like reading a detective story when someone has told you how it ends. To give the game away like this is, of course, to spoil any good story, and when the author himself lets you into the secret, he ruins his own plot. But what else could Mark do? He was writing to Christians who knew the end of the story, and who could not be kept in suspense. In such a situation, the only realistic policy is a bold one: if you cannot mystify your readers, then the next best thing is to make sure that they appreciate the intricacies of the plot! Now of course Mark's purpose was not to mystify his readers, but to help them to see the significance of the story he had to tell: but what he has written is a kind of detective story with the dénouement at the very beginning, to make sure that we recognize the significance of the blatant clues which he has scattered throughout his narrative.

But if the Markan prologue is indeed the key which explains what the rest of his Gospel is all about, then I suggest that we really ought to take it seriously as such, and recognize that Mark here is doing something different from what he does in the rest of his book. We need to examine the information about Jesus which he gives us here, and which he expects us to hold in our hands as a guide as we thread our way through the rest of his Gospel. The prologue therefore repays careful analysis, and we need to remember that here Mark is letting us into secrets which remain hidden, throughout most of the drama, from the great majority of the characters in the story.

I have started to speak about Mark's prologue as though it were like the Johannine prologue – which in fact is what it is: both serve as introductions and summaries of certain fundamental assumptions of the authors which contain the key to what follows. In his lectures on the Gospel of John one year, one of my colleagues startled his students by spending almost the whole year dealing with the prologue; by the end of the course, he had hardly moved beyond John 1.18. The reason, of course, is that those first few verses of John contain ideas which are worked out in the rest of the Gospel. In his own way, the same is true for Mark. Though John offers us philosophical reflection, and Mark a narrative account, both of them set out to tell us who Jesus is. John tells us that he is the Logos made flesh, and the Son of God. John also makes clear what is the relationship between Jesus and John the Baptist: the Baptist was sent to bear witness to the light, and he declares that after him comes one who ranks before him. Mark, also, tells us that Jesus is the Son of God, and he, too, makes clear the relationship between Jesus and John the Baptist: the Baptist bears witness to one who comes after him, and declares that he is unworthy to unfasten his successor's shoes.

The purpose of Mark's work is made plain in v. 1: he is writing the Gospel about Jesus Christ. This is Mark's own title, and he has a right to be heard. He is not writing a life of Jesus, nor is he editing a collection of anecdotes, but offering us the good news about Jesus. We shall, of course, expect Mark to give us information about what Jesus did and said, but ultimately the Gospel is based on *who* he is; it is this which explains why and how Jesus acts and speaks as he does. It is this information about who Jesus is that Mark gives us in vv. 1–13.

The rest of Mark's prologue falls into three short sections:

(*a*) 1.2–8. John the Baptist and his relationship to Jesus.
(*b*) 1.9–11. The baptism of Jesus.
(*c*) 1.12–13. The temptation of Jesus.

Let us look at these three sections in turn.

(*a*) *John the Baptist*

It is worth noting, first of all, what Mark does *not* tell us. There is in Mark no account of John's exhortation to social righteousness, as there is in Luke – no good advice to tax-gatherers and soldiers. The figure of John is completely subordinate to the main theme. This is seen in the way in which Mark introduces him into the narrative. In both Matthew and Luke, he is a character in the action, and is introduced as such. Matthew begins: 'In those days came John the Baptist'; Luke: 'In the fifteenth year of the reign of Tiberius Caesar . . . [and so on; then] . . . the word of God came to John the son of Zechariah in the wilderness.' Mark, on the other hand, simply introduces John with the phrase 'as it is written' and a couple of Old Testament quotations: for him, John is not an event in his own right, but merely the one who prepares the way. His importance lies only in his relationship to Jesus. The Old Testament quotations with which he is introduced tell us more about *Jesus* than about John. In their original contexts, these quotations from Mal. 3.1 and Isa. 40.3 both speak of one who prepares the way of the Lord. Mark, by changing the personal pronouns, makes 'the Lord' refer to Jesus. According to Malachi, the messenger is sent to prepare the way before the Lord comes with judgment, and the idea that the Lord would come in judgment is common enough elsewhere. John accordingly preaches repentance (v. 2); the response is that the whole country of Judaea and all who live in Jerusalem come for baptism. Mark's account has been described as hyperbole, but one should not dismiss his 'all's as pictorial exaggeration. John does not call for individual penitence but for national repentance: the way of the Lord can only be prepared if the whole nation is ready; the fact that the whole country and all the inhabitants of the capital respond to John's preaching demonstrates that his mission has been accomplished.

Later in the Gospel, in chapter 9, John is identified with the returning Elijah of Mal. 4.5; so that we do not miss the point, it is made clear for us here in the description of John's food and clothing in v. 6. The details of his frugal diet – surely he ate something more than honey and locusts! – and his uncomfortable garment are not, of course, given us as interesting or even memorable facts; they serve to identify him with Elijah as he is depicted in I Kings 1.8. The whole description of John is meant to give us the eschatological setting: the signs are all present; what comes next must be the long awaited salvation.

John the Baptist serves only to prepare the way – to point to one coming after him. This he does effectively in what he says in vv. 7–8, the only details which Mark gives us of his message: it is simply a contrast between himself and the one who comes after him, who is stronger than himself. The term 'stronger' is a strange one for him to use; we might have expected him to say 'greater'. But John points to the strong one – to the mighty one, who is the eschatological deliverer. The contrast is not only in strength, but in rank: John is unworthy even to perform the menial task of a slave – to take off his shoes and carry them. The contrast could not be greater, for this action was regarded as so degrading that no Jew would perform it for another. Finally, the contrast between them is seen in their actions: one has baptized with water; the other will baptize with Holy Spirit. What exactly John himself thought he was doing in the rite of baptism remains a puzzle. One thing is, however, certain – it was a sign of repentance. Probably it was linked with the custom of proselyte baptism; just as the Gentile convert needed baptism to cleanse him from uncleanness when he entered Israel, so the Jews needed cleansing as they repented and waited for the renewing of God's people. Whatever John was doing, Mark stresses its preparatory nature: baptism, like John himself, serves only to point forward to one who comes. Baptism with water and with Spirit serve to relate and contrast John and Jesus.

It is significant that the first thing that Mark tells us about Jesus is that he is to baptize men with the Spirit – significant, but also puzzling, since as far as the Gospel is concerned, although Jesus himself is clearly 'baptized with the Holy Spirit', this promise remains an unfulfilled prediction. Some have thought that Mark's Gospel originally concluded with an account of Pentecost.[5] But perhaps a better explanation is that baptism with the Spirit belongs to the period *after* the resurrection, which Mark does not describe. Possibly Christian experience of the Spirit was so much a present experience for Mark and his first readers that an account of its origin seemed unnecessary. Baptism with the Spirit (a phrase echoed only in I Cor. 12.13) is another eschatological feature, the fulfilment of the promise in Joel 2 that the Spirit of God will be poured out on all flesh. Its use here serves to emphasize both the link and the gap between John and Jesus: John prepares the way, but Jesus brings the final salvation.

(*b*) *The baptism*

Just as the narrative about John is used by Mark only in order to tell us something about Jesus, so the story of the baptism of Jesus himself is merely a setting for the revelation of his identity. The later evangelists seem to be somewhat embarrassed by the baptism, but not so Mark; it probably would not have occurred to him that there was any cause for embarrassment. The acceptance by Jesus of baptism at the hands of John is a necessary link between them, and an acknowledgment by Jesus of John's preparatory role. Moreover, the Messiah stands *with* his people, as well as over against them, and it is therefore essential that he join this eschatological movement – a movement which is concerned to break with Israel's past disobedience, and which looks for the kingdom of God. But the vital elements in this story are the opening of the heavens, the descent of the Spirit, and the voice of the Father.

The rending apart of the heavens is used in the Old Testament to signify the descent of God to earth to assist his people. It was an obvious and powerful metaphor in an age which thought in terms of a three-decker universe with God 'up there'. In Isa. 64.1, and in apocryphal writings, it is used of the eschatological salvation when God will finally deliver his people. The descent of the Spirit, equally, is an eschatological event. The Jew of the first century AD thought of the activity of God's Spirit as belonging to the past and to the future, but not the present. In the past, the Spirit had been active in the creation of the world, in history, and in the lives of particular men with special gifts. But with the end of prophecy the Spirit had withdrawn from Israel; the next manifestation would be that which marked God's final salvation of his people, when the Messiah was given the Spirit. The descent of the Spirit on Jesus is therefore an eschatological event. Mark spells out for us here the theological truth which Luke summed up later in Acts 10.38: 'God anointed Jesus of Nazareth with the Holy Spirit and with power.'

All four evangelists tell us that the Spirit descends on Jesus like a dove, and we may safely conclude that they regard this comparison as significant; our problem is in knowing what this significance was! They are using symbols whose meaning is no longer clear to us. The suggestion that the dove represents Israel does not explain why it is used here to symbolize the Spirit. Perhaps the clue is to be found in later rabbinic writings which interpret Gen. 1.1 by speaking of the Holy Spirit brooding over the waters at the creation like a dove brooding over her young.[6] If Mark was aware of this symbolism, then what he is portraying is the creative spirit of God at work once again in the world – in the person of Jesus. Such an idea should not surprise us, for the thought of a new or restored creation is a thoroughly biblical one, and it had been taken up already by St Paul, who thought of redemption in terms of a new creation brought about in Christ through the work of the Spirit.[7]

Now if in using this symbol of the dove Mark was reminding us in particular of the creative activity of the Spirit of God, then it is interesting to note that this story of Jesus' baptism expresses the same truth which is to be found in the narratives with which both Matthew and Luke have chosen to open their Gospels; for they have traced the activity of the creative Spirit further back, and shown that God was at work in the birth of Jesus. Both the birth and the baptism of Jesus demonstrate the new, creative activity of the Spirit. Finally, we may observe that we have another parallel with the Johannine Prologue, since the opening words of John 1 link what happens through Jesus with the creative power of God by repeating the opening phrase of the book of Genesis: 'in the beginning'.

Whether or not I am right about the symbolism of the dove, it is clear that Mark believed that the knowledge that the Spirit had come upon Jesus was of vital importance for our understanding of who he is and what he does. The descent of the Spirit is not a transitory experience, but the explanation of the events that are to follow.

The voice which comes from heaven in v. 11 is consistently described by commentators in terms of the *bath qol,* an idea known to us from the writings of the rabbis. The *bath qol* (literally 'daughter of the voice') was said to be the echo of God's voice, and was thought to have been heard by some of the holy rabbis who, had they lived in an earlier and worthier age, might have been granted the privilege of hearing God's voice directly. Clearly, then, the *bath qol* was at best a second-rate thing, a substitute for the real voice of God which had spoken in the past to prophets, but now was heard no longer. It seems to me misleading to interpret the voice at the baptism in terms of the *bath qol*, for the evangelists certainly had no intention of describing Jesus as the recipient of a second-class revelation by means of something which was only a substitute! Mark has just told us that the heavens have been rent asunder and the Spirit of God has descended on Jesus. The barrier dividing God and man has been torn aside: there is no need for a secondary relaying system to be used, for the Messiah has been anointed with God's own Spirit, and God speaks to him directly.

The voice from heaven announces who Jesus is. The words are addressed to Jesus, and there is no hint that they are heard by anyone else, either by John or by the crowds. Only we, the readers of the Gospel, are allowed to overhear them, and are let into the secret of Jesus' identity. Jesus is addressed as God's beloved (or only) Son. The phrase is used in the Old Testament of Isaac, who was Abraham's only son. The address to Jesus, 'You are . . .', echoes the words of Ps. 2.7, where Israel's king is acknowledged as God's son. In the course of the pages that follow Jesus will be addressed by different people in different ways. Some will get him right and some will get him wrong, but there can be no argument about the truth of words uttered from heaven. Mark clearly means us to see this as the truth about Jesus – not a half-truth, or a misunderstanding, as some human confessions about Jesus turn out to be, but the full truth, spoken with divine authority. This, according to Mark, is who Jesus is: we will do well to hold on to it, as a statement of crucial importance.

This story is often treated as an account of Jesus' own self-awareness – perhaps as the moment when he first understood the truth about himself and his mission. Did Mark perhaps understand it that way? We cannot be sure. If he did, then this was certainly not his main point, for his concern was not to record Jesus' spiritual biography, but to help us to understand the gospel. We cannot use this story to try to recover Jesus' experience and feelings: it is primarily a christological statement, which will enable us to understand the rest of Mark's book. Jesus is the one on whom the Spirit rests, the one who has God's approval, the one who is uniquely Son of God.

(*c*) *The temptation*

The final section in Mark's prologue is the story of the temptation of Jesus. This story, too, has often been used by those would-be biographers of Jesus who have attempted to reconstruct his religious experience. Some have interpreted it as the inevitable reaction which follows a great spiritual experience, the trough which succeeds exaltation. Others have seen it, as the accounts in Matthew and Luke suggest, as the deliberation by Jesus on the exact messianic role which he was to follow, as God's anointed one. It may well be that each of these interpretations is in some measure true, but we should banish them both from our minds in trying to understand Mark's account of the temptation, for he is not concerned with either of them. His interest is still christological: his purpose is to tell us something further about the person of Jesus – namely that his ministry is to be understood in terms of a cosmic battle between Jesus and Satan. The importance of this event is underlined by the introductory words in v. 12, where it is said that the Spirit drove Jesus into the wilderness; this would be a strange feature of the narrative if Mark were thinking, as the author to the Hebrews did, of a temptation in all points like ours. But this temptation is *not* a temptation like ours, for it is a battle between the Messiah and Satan, between the Spirit of God and the power of evil.[8] Once again Mark is describing an eschatological event – the joining of the great eschatological battle. The Spirit drives Jesus into the wilderness, not merely that he may get away from the madding crowd, but because the wilderness is the home of demons. It is not simply that Jesus is attacked and tempted by Satan: Jesus is compelled by the Spirit of God, and it is Jesus who is on the offensive, who is taking the battle into the enemy camp. He is supported in the fight by angels who serve him – not, in the Marcan account, after the event (as in Matthew), but apparently throughout the campaign; Mark makes no mention of fasting. The presence of the wild beasts is probably another eschatological feature. The Messiah remains in safety among them. Wild beasts are sometimes associated with demons in Jewish thought, and it may be that Mark sees them as supporters of Satan, now crushed by the Messiah. Psalm 91 couples service by the angels with a promise that lions and serpents will be trampled underfoot. Or perhaps we should understand the presence of the animals (and of the angels) in terms of the restoration of the harmony of nature which is yet another feature of the eschatological scene. The two ideas are in fact allied, for the revolt of the animal kingdom against man was seen by the Jews as part of the corruption of nature which followed the Fall, the result of the work of Satan in the world, so that Satan's defeat will mean that nature is restored to order. If the ideas seem fanciful, it is because we no longer think, as Mark and his contemporaries did, of a world dominated by demons, and the hope of Paradise regained on earth is one which finally died out some time between the two world wars. But to Mark's first readers, his meaning would be clear enough: the Messiah has joined battle with Satan, and the final struggle has begun; the overthrow of Satan and the restoration of mankind are at hand.

So we come to the end of Mark's prologue. We are now in possession of the vital information about Jesus which will enable us to comprehend the meaning of the drama which unfolds in the rest of the book. We know that Jesus is the one whose coming was announced in the pages of the Old Testament, who brings salvation to Israel; that he stands in a unique relationship to God and enjoys divine favour, and that the Spirit of God is at work in him; that he has done battle with Satan. One thing Mark has *not* told us – and that is the outcome of the battle between Jesus and Satan! Perhaps it seemed unnecessary to him to spell out that Jesus was the victor; perhaps he saw the whole of Jesus' ministry as a blow-by-blow defeat of Satan; at any rate, in the pages that follow, Mark leaves us in no doubt about the result of the conflict.

Two things bind the three sections of the prologue together: one is their setting – all of them take place in the wilderness; the other is the Holy Spirit. The references to the Spirit are the more striking when we remember that there are very few indeed in the rest of the Gospel – the only important one being in a discussion between Jesus and his opponents in chapter 3 in which Satan also reappears. Yet clearly for Mark, the Spirit is an important key to understanding the person and work of Jesus. He has told us that Jesus will baptize with the Spirit, that he himself has already been baptized with the Spirit, and that it is in the power of the Spirit that he has done battle with Satan. If references to the Spirit are rare in the rest of the Gospel, this is not because Mark loses interest in the idea, but because these first few verses are a kind of theological commentary on the rest of the narrative. In v. 14 we come down to earth with a bump, and the characters in the story become the normal, everyday inhabitants of Galilee. It is as though in vv. 1–13, Mark has allowed us to see Jesus from God's angle, and now the curtain falls, and we are among men and women who stumble around, wondering what is happening. But though the characters in the story are bewildered, Mark does not intend us to forget the truth which he has uncovered in these opening verses. From time to time in the course of the narrative he will nudge his readers, reminding them of the true significance of what is going on. Like a Greek chorus explaining the meaning of events in a play, he will make sure that we, at least, realize that the story he unfolds is good news about the Son of God, in whom God's Spirit is at work.

TWO

'Like Pearls on a String'

According to the well-known tradition recorded by Papias in the second century, Mark was the interpreter of Peter, and wrote down accurately all that he could remember of the things said and done by the Lord – but not in order. By 'not in order' Papias presumably meant 'not in chronological order'. Anxious as he was to give the Gospel some kind of apostolic authority, he nevertheless felt that Mark's arrangement was haphazard and muddled.

It is perhaps this apparent lack of order that has been to some extent responsible for the relative unpopularity of Mark's Gospel in the past. By contrast, Matthew presents his material in a much neater and more ordered manner. Yet possibly as a result of his lack of precision, Mark does produce an extremely dynamic portrait of Jesus. His abruptness of style, his constant repetition of the words 'and' and 'immediately', his broken constructions and his use of the historic present, are all features that tend to be despised by the grammarians, who speak of Mark's barbarous Greek, but which nevertheless contribute to the dynamic force of the book. These characteristics are at once the result of Mark's own rapid thought, and the means by which he produces the sense of rapid action, so conveying a sense of dramatic tension.

But if Mark did *not* write things 'in order', then how *did* he set to work? Did he, as Papias implies, just jot things down as they occurred to him? Such, apparently, was the view of those scholars who described the individual units in Mark's Gospel as being arranged 'like pearls on a string'.

But we have already seen that this description suggests something rather more careful and selective than those who used it imagined. There are, moreover, indications that Mark has placed the material precisely where it is for very good reasons. There are signs, that is, that Mark has selected and arranged his pearls with considerable care. Can we discover the design he had in mind?

One answer to this question very popular until recently was offered by C. H. Dodd. In a well-known article published some fifty years ago,[1] Professor Dodd argued that in addition to a collection of material about Jesus – stories of miracles, other incidents, small collections of sayings and so on – Mark possessed a brief outline of the ministry of Jesus, which had been handed down to him via the tradition of the church. Mark used this historical outline as the framework of his Gospel – the string on which he threaded his pearls – and on it he hung the rest of his material.[2] In other words, the Markan order of events is, after all, basically historical.

The weaknesses of this theory were ruthlessly exposed by D. E. Nineham, in an essay written some twenty-five years later.[3] His chief criticism of Dodd's theory was that the traditional outline of Jesus' ministry which it presupposed could have had no usefulness to the early church, and that there is therefore no likelihood that it would have been preserved. Moreover, even if it *did* exist, and even if it *was* used by Mark, this outline, as reconstructed by Dodd, is far too brief and general for it to be useful as a chronological guide: the framework is too vague and sketchy to provide a firm chronological setting for the material. This is the really significant step in Professor Nineham's argument: the summary outline of Jesus' ministry suggested by Dodd did not give sufficient indications as to where material 'belongs' to be of any real importance. It certainly did not provide for modern scholars the chronological framework of Jesus' ministry which Dodd had hoped for; but neither did it suggest that Mark himself was primarily interested in arranging his material in chronological order, for it offered little more than statements that Jesus taught, or healed, or cast out unclean spirits.

We must, of course, be careful to distinguish here between two quite separate questions. On the one hand, there is the question that primarily concerned Professors Dodd and Nineham: this was the question whether Mark's ordering of events could be treated as a reliable chronological outline of the ministry of Jesus. In thinking about Mark's christology, however, we are more concerned with the second question – did Mark consider chronology *important*? And it looks very much as though he did not have sufficient information to make chronology an important factor in arranging some, at least, of his material. Not only is Dodd's suggested historical outline extremely sketchy, but almost all the individual units in Mark's story lack any kind of chronological detail. Only rarely is there something that links one story with another. Were our imaginary necklace to break, there would be nothing to show where each bead 'belonged'. The tradition came to Mark piecemeal; each story had been told and retold in the church community for its own sake, and had no kind of date label attached to it. Mark's retelling of the story certainly does not suggest that he is interested in the chronology of particular incidents; with rare and significant exceptions, he is content to introduce events with a vague 'in those days' or a simple 'and'.

It would be foolish to deny that Mark is concerned with history, or that he intends to record divine action at work in history. Mark has presented his 'gospel' to us in the form of an historical narrative: like the writers of the Old Testament, he sees a relationship between God's saving activity and historical events. The form critics have emphasized the fact that the oral tradition used by Mark was largely fragmentary, or else arranged topically; they have denied the existence of an historical outline of Jesus' ministry. It is all the more significant, then, that Mark has chosen to present his

Gospel in the form of an historical narrative. For clearly he might have followed some other form. He might have arranged his material entirely on a topical basis, and told us: these are the things that Jesus said; these are the miracles that he performed; this is how he came to choose disciples and to send them out; this is how he fell foul of the religious and political authorities and was put to death. But this was not Mark's way; he chose to present his Gospel in the form of an outline of the ministry of Jesus, from his first proclamation of the kingdom in Galilee to the climax of the story in Jerusalem. Though Mark's Gospel is not a biography of Jesus, it is understandable why so many readers have treated it as though it were, for its broad outlines, if no more, are chronological.

There is, then, an historical framework of a kind in Mark's Gospel, but it is by no means sufficiently extensive or sufficiently rigid to explain the selection and placing of all his material. How, then, was this process governed? Did Mark simply use the material available to him like a lucky dip? Or can we discover the motives that led him to place it as he has? Until fairly recently, most scholars tended either to cling to Dodd's thesis, and believe that Mark was attempting to arrange the material chronologically, or to think his arrangement haphazard. But in the last twenty years or so, more and more have been convinced that Mark's ordering is deliberate, and that it reflects his theological concerns. This change in attitude coincides with the rise in scholarly circles of redaction criticism, which is concerned with the way in which the evangelists edited the material in order to express their understanding of the gospel, and to stress those implications of the gospel which they felt needed special emphasis. In other words, all the evangelists are now being treated as theologians in their own right, who had a gospel to preach, and who were concerned to relate that gospel to the needs of their communities, just as Paul, the most famous of evangelists, had done before them. In asking why Mark arranged the material as he did, therefore, we are not thinking of him manipulating the evidence to suit his own ends, or to pursue some particular theological bee in his bonnet; we are thinking of him primarily as a pastor, who was concerned to deal with the particular needs and problems (and perhaps failings) of the community or congregation for whom he was writing.

But how do we 'do' redaction criticism? How do we decide what motives led each evangelist to write as he did, and to organize his material in the way that he has? More specifically, how do we do this in the case of Mark? In order to trace the process of redaction, we need to be able to compare the end product with the raw materials – the final version of a Gospel with the sources which the evangelist used. This is one reason why old-fashioned source criticism is still of vital importance. If we can assume the priority of Mark, and a lost document used by Matthew and Luke which we may for convenience call Q, then we may perhaps be able to discover what Matthew and Luke have done with their sources. Unfortunately, of course, things are not so simple. The priority of Mark is under renewed attack; the shape of Q, if it ever existed, is unclear; we do not know what other sources Matthew and Luke may have used. But when we turn to Mark, then our problems multiply. For if Mark was the first Gospel to be written (and this still seems to be the most likely hypothesis), then we have no sources with which to compare it. How, then, are we to decide how he has used and adapted the material? Clearly we can only do so by examining the Gospel itself, and following up the clues that we find there.

First of all, we can take note of the material that Mark has chosen to include. Once we abandon the assumption that Mark made use of every piece of tradition known to him, it becomes plain that he has exercised a certain choice in making use of some material and excluding other pieces. Not so long ago, one used to read arguments for the priority of Mark which ran: 'How could Mark have failed to make use of the Lord's Prayer or the Beatitudes, had he known them?' The answer, of course, as we now see it is, 'Quite easily – if they did not fit his purpose.' There is no reason to assume that Mark made use of everything he knew – or that certain pieces of tradition which have been hallowed by centuries of Christian usage would necessarily have had the same appeal for him as they have for us. There is every reason to assume that he made a conscious choice. The problem, of course, is that we have no means of knowing what he rejected; we certainly cannot conclude that tradition used in the other Gospels but which is missing from Mark has been deliberately left out. But if he has chosen to include certain traditions, then this suggests that he considered this material important and relevant.

Secondly, we may take note of the order in which Mark has placed the material. Now there are two obvious problems here. The first is to know whether or not Mark is in fact responsible for the ordering of the material. Some of it may have come to him in blocks, and the order may therefore be the work of someone before Mark. There is, for example, a group of conflict stories in chapter 2. It is often assumed that Mark took these over en bloc, and that someone else had already grouped the sayings together; if so, then clearly we cannot argue anything from Mark's placing of the stories together. But this assumption is a somewhat strange one. Why should anyone *need* a group of conflict stories? What purpose would such a collection serve? May it not be Mark himself who has placed the stories together, in order to show how the Jewish authorities refused to accept the authority of Jesus? This seems to me to be a much more likely explanation of the ordering of the material – but clearly we must be careful not to assume too much, lest we attribute to Mark what is in fact the work of someone else. Again, it is generally assumed that the passion narrative had already been put together as a continuous narrative long before Mark wrote his Gospel. It is worth asking whether in fact it might have been the work of Mark himself, and whether this might tell us something about his purpose; but again, we must be very careful not to assume too much. How, then, are we to know where Mark has been at work? The most obvious cases will be those where Mark betrays his hand by doing the same thing more than once. And the most obvious example of this is the way in which he links two stories by sandwiching them together, intercalating one into the other – for example the well-known case in chapter 5 where the story of the woman with the haemorrhage is told in the middle of that of the raising of Jairus' daughter. This kind of thing happens so often that it must almost certainly be Mark's handiwork. The other problem with studying the order of the material is that there is a great temptation to see patterns where perhaps none were intended. The patterns which Austin Farrer[4] found in Mark's Gospel, for example, were fascinating – but were they intentional or accidental? Similarly, the links which Michael Goulder[5] finds with his hypothetical synagogue lectionary may well be fortuitous, and not the features that led Mark to arrange the material as he did.

Thirdly, we may compare the Markan tradition with parallel traditions in other sources, where these exist. Unfortunately, of course, this will not be very often, but sometimes we are lucky enough to find a 'Q' version of a saying that we have in Mark, and the Markan version will not necessarily be the earlier. But again, of course, we must beware of assuming that alterations have necessarily been made by Mark; they may be due to those who handled the material before him.

Finally, we must pay careful attention to any adaptations in the material that *have* been made by Mark. And though we may not have Mark's sources, we may be able to detect these adaptations by paying careful attention to Mark's vocabulary and style. Once again, we must be careful not to jump to conclusions. The fact that Mark is particularly fond of certain words or expressions does not preclude the possibility that others may have used those words and expressions before him. But quirks of style *can* betray an author. It is well-known that Mark was particularly fond of using the word *euthus*, immediately. A sentence that begins 'and immediately' is not necessarily Markan, but it certainly stands a good chance of having been written, or at least adapted, by Mark.

At this point it is well to remind ourselves of the conclusions we reached in examining Mark's 'prologue'. If those introductory paragraphs do indeed provide a key for understanding the rest of the Gospel, then they should help us in trying to see how Mark has arranged his material. Mark began by telling us that he was offering us 'the gospel about Jesus Christ, the Son of God', and he then spelt out, in two short paragraphs, the witness of John, of scripture, of the Spirit and of the divine voice, that Jesus was indeed the Christ and Son of God. We shall not go far wrong if we assume that Mark's purpose in the rest of his book is to spell out the meaning of that gospel about Jesus, and to show us the impact that Jesus has on men and women. In other words, his purpose is primarily christological: he aims to show us who Jesus is.

One way in which he does this is in his arrangement of Jesus' teaching. It has often been pointed out that, though Mark refers frequently to the fact that Jesus taught, he includes comparatively little of Jesus' teaching. We must be careful not to be led astray by this statement, for if we were to add up all the sections of teaching, together with the individual sayings attributed to Jesus, we should find that they amounted to a considerable proportion of the Gospel. Nevertheless, it is true that there are far fewer parables in Mark than in Matthew and Luke, and certainly nothing to compare with the Sermon on the Mount or the Sermon on the Plain – or, of course, with the Johannine Discourses. The popular explanation for this used to be that Matthew and Luke had access to material that was not available to Mark; commentators found it incredible that Mark should have omitted some of the priceless teaching found in the other Gospels if it was in fact known to him. But can we be sure that this other material was unkown to him? Did he (as Papias said) write down 'all that he remembered' – or all that was available to him – without discrimination? Or could it be that the parable of the Prodigal Son and the Beatitudes, to take two obvious examples, just were not relevant to his particular purpose? Since Mark has not told us the answer to this question, we cannot be definite, but if we find that all the teaching of Jesus which Mark *does* give us points in the same direction, then we shall perhaps be justified in assuming that he has been more selective than is sometimes supposed.

And when we examine this material, then we discover that in a quite remarkable way it *does* point in one direction – namely at Jesus himself. For although Jesus never preaches directly about himself, nevertheless the result of the way in which Mark has presented his teaching is to make it witness to Jesus. Let us see how this is achieved.

The first mention of the teaching of Jesus comes at the very beginning of the story, in 1.15, where Jesus comes into Galilee preaching the gospel of God, and saying: 'The time is fulfilled, and the kingdom of God is at hand; repent, and believe in the gospel.' Mark might not have agreed with the commentator who wrote that Jesus and the kingdom are here identified, but he would certainly have agreed that the two are closely bound up together.[6] Since this declaration follows immediately after the prologue, we can hardly fail to link the statement that the time is fulfilled and the kingdom is at the door with what we have just been told about Jesus himself. Jesus does not simply announce the kingdom's coming; he brings it.

The next reference to teaching comes a few verses later,

where we are told that Jesus entered the synagogue on the sabbath and taught. In v. 15 we were given a two-line summary of Jesus' message – this time we are told nothing at all about its content. The whole emphasis in this incident is concentrated on the reaction of Jesus' hearers, who are astonished at his teaching, because 'he taught them as one who had authority, and not as the scribes' (v. 22). In contrast to the local scribes, who passed on the teaching that they themselves had received, Jesus taught as one with first-hand knowledge and authority. In the incident that follows, the teaching of Jesus is not only described as 'new', but is linked with his authority over unclean spirits. For Mark, the contrast between the teaching of the scribes and the teaching of Jesus points to the contrast between the old order of things and the new, between the traditions of men and the power of God. Remembering what we have read in the prologue, we realize that the authority of Jesus is to be traced to the Spirit of God, whose power is working through him.

In the chapters that follow we have several references to the fact that Jesus taught. We also have a number of conflict stories which feature sayings of Jesus. Leaving these aside for the moment, we come to the first main section of teaching, which is found in chapter 4. This opens with the parable of the Sower, the explanation of which, in v. 13, opens with the significant words: 'Do you not understand this parable? How then will you understand all the parables?' Clearly Mark regarded this introductory parable as the key to understanding the rest. It is significant that now that Mark has at last paused to draw breath and to give us the content of Jesus' teaching, the first thing he gives us is not the teaching itself but teaching *about* teaching, a parable about parables. And to make quite sure we understand, he gives us not only the parable itself but an explanation of the parable, making a 'sandwich' of the two by joining them together with a conversation on the theme of parables between Jesus and his disciples in vv. 10–12. It is, indeed, a matter of irony that Mark has made his own understanding of parables so plain, and yet commentators have frequently refused to believe that he can really mean what he says. Many have thought it incredible that Mark could really have believed that the purpose of the parables was to conceal the truth and to prevent repentance; but other explanations of v. 12 are unconvincing. Whatever Jesus himself may have said and may have meant in using this quotation from Isaiah – and that is another matter – it is well-nigh impossible to escape the conclusion that Mark believed that the purpose of the parables was to hide the truth from those whose hearts were already hardened. The question – Why then did Jesus teach the people at all, instead of concentrating his attention on the disciples? – receives its answer in this parable of the Sower: such is God's method. Mark would no doubt have agreed with the saying in John 15.22 that those who have heard Jesus are now without excuse. Mark's attitude arises from the fact that he looks back on the ministry of Jesus in the double conviction that Jesus was the Messiah, and that what happened to him in the course of that ministry must have been in accordance with God's almighty purposes. We must return later to the problem raised by the notion that the truth is deliberately hidden from men and women, but for the moment it is enough for our purpose to note Mark's conviction that the hearers of Jesus are divided into two camps *through hearing him*. On the one hand there are those to whom the secret of the kingdom of God has been given; on the other, there are those 'outside', to whom everything is obscure. Mankind is divided into two, and they are divided by the response they make to Jesus; for it is to his disciples, those who accept the authority of Jesus, that the secret of the kingdom is given, and it is those outside his company from whom the truth remains hidden.

This contrast, which is stated so bluntly in vv. 11–12, is spelt out again in the explanation of the parable in vv. 13–

20. How close this explanation is to the intention of Jesus, and whether he himself used allegory, need not concern us now. It is clear that Mark understood the parable to be about the teaching of Jesus and its results. The existence of four groups of hearers should not disguise from us the fact that basically there are only two: there are those whose hearing of the word of Jesus bears fruit, and there are those whose hearing does not bear fruit. Mankind is divided into two, and they are divided by the very fact of hearing Jesus. On the one hand stand those who hear and understand the word of Jesus – the gospel – and on the other stand those on whom the word makes no lasting impression. The fact that the second group is here subdivided into three is perhaps more than simply an example of the art of the storyteller; for it emphasizes the dangers that beset the growing seed. But we should also note the nature of the opposition: in the first case it is Satan who takes away the seed as soon as it is sown; in the second, tribulation and persecution on account of the word defeat the growing seed; in the third, it is choked by the cares of the world, by delight in riches and other desires. Although Satan is named as the culprit in the first case only, he is undoubtedly seen as the cause of the opposition which eventually overcomes the other groups also: tribulation and persecution on account of the word are part of Satan's opposition to the activity of Christ; cares and desires and delight in riches are all part of what we may perhaps term Satan's normal routine. So in the teaching of Jesus, as in the rest of his activity, we see a battle being waged between Jesus and Satan. The teaching of Jesus must be seen against the background of the cosmic warfare which began in 1.13. The two groups formed in response to his teaching correspond to the two sides in this battle: by their response to Jesus' teaching, men and women have taken sides in what amounts to a gigantic tug-of-war between the two protagonists. On the one side God, working through Jesus, gives the secret of the kingdom to those who have

become disciples, and grants understanding to those who have ears to hear. On the other side Satan, working through persecution and the lure of this world, endeavours to prevent the word from bearing fruit.

The explanation of the parable of the Sower is followed by four short sayings which Mark – or possibly someone before him – has joined together (vv. 21–5). In this context, they serve to emphasize two contrasts: one is between those who have and those who do not have – between those who understand and those who do not; the other is between what is hidden and what is revealed. The emphasis in this second contrast seems to be on what is hidden now but will ultimately be revealed, and this is brought out in the two parables of the kingdom with which Mark concludes the chapter. These parables are essentially concerned with contrast: the contrast between the seed sown by the farmer and the field of corn which it produces; between the tiny mustard seed and the tree which grows from it. The meaning of these parables for Mark is not to be found either in the traditional interpretation which emphasized the time of the church as a long period of growth, nor in Dodd's theory of 'realized eschatology', which declares that the harvest has come in the ministry of Jesus.[7] For Mark, the messiahship of Jesus is hidden during his ministry, and the meaning of his teaching is also hidden, except to those to whom God reveals it. The kingdom is displayed in the life of Jesus – but it is displayed like seed thrown on to the earth: you do not know that it is there unless you are let into the secret. But what the kingdom *will* be is a very different matter; its greatness comes by the power of God – as silent and mysterious and effective as the power of growth, which causes the earth to produce 'of itself'.

This collection of parables in chapter 4 provides the longest section in Mark of teaching addressed by Jesus to the crowds. We have remarked how little actual teaching Mark includes, compared with the large number of parables in Matthew and Luke, and the discourses in John.[8] This is partly due, of course, to the brevity of Mark's Gospel: the total proportion of teaching in relation to other material is considerable. Moreover, Mark constantly emphasizes Jesus' role as teacher, even when he does not describe the content of his teaching.[9] This emphasis, together with the particular parables that Mark has chosen to include, means that the material all stresses one particular theme: Jesus proclaims the kingdom of God, and calls on men and women to respond to his call. If much of the teaching that is familiar to us from the other Gospels is missing from Mark, this is perhaps because it would not have served his purpose, which is to confront his readers with the all-important question regarding their response to Jesus.

Mark's next reference to the teaching of Jesus occurs in chapter 6, where Jesus returns to his native town and teaches in the synagogue on the sabbath. Once again, we see the terrible result that his teaching has when men's hearts are hardened, and when they have no ears to hear. For Mark, it is never true that the words of Jesus have no effect: men either receive them, or they refuse to believe, as they do here.

By the time we reach the incident at Caesarea Philippi, therefore, at the end of chapter 8, the passage which is commonly regarded as the turning-point in Mark's Gospel – the teaching addressed by Jesus to the crowds has served to divide them into two camps. From this point onwards, his teaching is of two kinds: on the one hand, we have teaching addressed to disciples or to would-be disciples; on the other hand, we have teaching which takes place in the context of conflict stories, which is addressed to his opponents, whose hearts have been hardened. The teaching given to the disciples is concerned primarily with the twin themes of the nature of Jesus' own role and mission and the meaning of discipleship – twin themes because the two belong together, and the second depends on the first. We must come back to these in later chapters. For the moment we notice simply that Mark tells us that Jesus taught the disciples 'plainly' or 'openly' (8.32). His comment underlines what is for Mark an important feature of Jesus' teaching. However uncomprehending the disciples may be, this is not because Jesus does not explain things to them clearly: the crowds are given only parables, since they are incapable of accepting more, but the disciples have the truth explained to them (4.33f.). So it is not surprising if, in this second part of the Gospel, where Mark concentrates on the teaching Jesus gives to the disciples, there are few parables; the couple used in chapter 13 have their meaning fully spelt out. The one parable told at length is that of the vineyard tenants in chapter 12. This time there is no lack of comprehension on the part of those to whom it is addressed; the religious authorities 'perceived that he had told the parable against them' (v. 12). The crowds may reject the teaching of Jesus because the truth is hidden from them, but the religious authorities have no such excuse. And if they realize that the parable is directed against them, should they not realize also the truth that is so plain to Mark and to his readers that the 'beloved Son' in the parable is none other than Jesus himself? Possibly Mark believes that the religious authorities did indeed recognize the implicit messianic claim in the parable – but nevertheless determined to destroy Jesus; like the scribes from Jerusalem who come to assess Jesus in 3.20–30, they see the truth and call it a lie. And the truth that is set out in this parable is once again the truth about Jesus: it is an attack by Jesus on the religious authorities, but as Mark tells it – rounding off the story with the promise of resurrection in vv. 10f. – the focal point of the story is Jesus himself.

We have seen already that the teaching of Jesus divides men and women into two groups: those few who respond by becoming disciples stand over against the crowds, who in various ways reject the truth. What divides them one from another is their attitude to Jesus himself, for either they are of his company or they are 'outside'. The same note is sounded again and again throughout the teaching given to the disciples. The loyalty he demands from his disciples means the willingness to follow his way of suffering (8.34); allegiance to the name of Jesus becomes all important – but it means following his example (9.33–41); those who seek to enter the kingdom must abandon all and follow Jesus (10. 17–31). Directly or indirectly, this teaching reminds us of the importance of the response we make to Jesus. Even when it is not specifically about Jesus – as with the parable of the Sower in chapter 4 – Mark's arrangement of his material means that he confronts his readers with the question: how do *you* respond to this Jesus? Are you for him or against him?

But there is in Mark a third group of men who, though we must include them among those who fail to respond to Jesus, are nevertheless to be distinguished from the crowd since, unlike them, they are not willing even to listen to Jesus. From the very beginning of Mark's story the religious authorities are opposed to Jesus, and throughout the narrative they take Satan's part. So antagonistic are they that it can hardly be said that Jesus teaches them, but there are many stories in which Jesus comes into conflict with them and which contain sayings of Jesus. There is, for example, the group of five so-called 'conflict stories' at the very beginning of the Gospel. I have suggested already that Mark himself may be responsible for grouping them together, and certainly when all five are read, one after another, they make an impact on the reader that suggests that they are not found side by side by chance. It is worth noting the claims that they contain:

'The Son of man has authority on earth to forgive sins' (2.10);
'I came not to call the righteous, but sinners' (2.17);

'Can the wedding guests fast while the bridegroom is with them' (2.19);
'The Son of man is lord even of the sabbath' (2.28);
'Is it lawful on the sabbath to do good or to do harm, to save life or to kill?' (3.4).

It is noticeable that every one of these sayings is about the authority of Jesus: this is for Mark the issue behind all the conflicts between Jesus and his opponents. The claims of Jesus are spelt out one by one – and the Jewish leaders refuse to accept them. In other words, this group of stories as used by Mark is essentially christological – it challenges his readers by underlining the authority which Jesus assumes in various aspects of his mission. He has the authority to forgive sins (the prerogative of God alone) – indeed, he has come into the world to call sinners. His presence is like that of the bridegroom, without whom there can be no joy. He is lord of the sabbath; he is not chained by the restrictions of the law. In contrast to his enemies, who do harm and destroy life, he does good and saves life. The reason for this is spelt out in 3.22–30, where we are reminded that the power at work in Jesus is that of the Holy Spirit – and the power at work in his enemies is that of Satan.

In three different contexts, therefore – addressing the crowds, instructing disciples, confronting opposition – the teaching of Jesus as presented by Mark has a remarkable unity and consistency. Though Jesus proclaims the kingdom and its coming, not himself, the effect of his teaching is to impress us with the authority of Jesus himself. By his arrangement and presentation of the material, Mark makes quite sure that his readers understand that the gospel in which Jesus calls men to believe (1.15) is in fact the gospel about Jesus Christ, the Son of God (1.1).

THREE

Signs and Wonders

One of the most striking things about Mark's Gospel is the amount of space that he devotes to Jesus' miracles. Clearly Mark considered them important, for he would not have given them the prominence that they have if he had not regarded them as significant. The fact that Mark found these stories in the tradition indicates that the church before him had also seen them as relevant and important. The questions we have to ask are: Why did Mark regard them as so important for the gospel about Jesus? What truth did he think they conveyed?

The miracle stories in Mark fall into two broad groups: apart from the general summaries of Jesus' activity, which refer to large numbers of people being healed, we have thirteen miracles of healing which are described in some detail, and five so-called 'nature' miracles. The healing miracles can be divided again into a further two groups: the first consists of exorcisms, and the second of other healings, which are perhaps best described as restorations. Let us look first at the exorcisms.

The very first miracle in the Gospel falls into this category, for it is the account in 1.23–28 of the man with an unclean spirit who confronts Jesus in the synagogue at Capernaum. The story is a typical account of an exorcism: the demon recognizes Jesus and speaks to him; he, in turn, rebukes the demon, commands it to be silent and expels it. The demon obeys, and the final convulsion and cry of his victim show that the exorcism has been effective; the miracle ends with the astonishment of the onlookers. There are, however, some features in this narrative that make it of particular interest. First, in Mark's account the exorcism is closely linked with the teaching that Jesus gives in the synagogue, which amazes his hearers by its authority. It is apparently while Jesus is teaching that the unclean spirit protests; and at the end of the narrative, Mark links the crowd's astonishment at the exorcism with their astonishment at the teaching.[1] The teaching of Jesus and his power over unclean spirits are seen as facets of one event: both are carried out with authority, for Jesus speaks as one who expects to be obeyed. The second interesting feature in this story is the way in which the unclean spirit addresses Jesus. As is often the case in exorcism narratives, the recognition of Jesus by the unclean spirit is spontaneous. The man has not been brought for healing to Jesus – indeed, in Mark's Gospel Jesus is not yet known as a healer – but simply reacts to his presence and teaching in this alarming way. But it is apparently the unclean spirit who is most alarmed, for he not only recognizes who Jesus is – the Holy One of God – but also realizes what he is doing: 'Why are you interfering with us? You have come to destroy us.' The use of the plural suggests that this one representative of the supernatural world speaks for the whole host of demons who are now confronted by the power of God in Jesus. He is the Holy One of God; he has come, not merely to deal with one unclean spirit, but to destroy the whole army of unclean spirits who serve their master, Satan. Already, at the beginning of Jesus' ministry, we see the significance of Jesus' fight with Satan: the defeat of the general means the rout of the troops. The *unclean* spirits are being destroyed by the *Holy* One of God, who is armed with the power of the Spirit of God.

The next references to exorcisms are general ones: Jesus heals many – Mark cannot tell us about them all. The summaries of healing miracles include references to demons and unclean spirits, who never fail to recognize Jesus, and who are silenced by him.[2] These accounts prepare us for the next passage we need to examine, in 3.21–35. This is, in fact, not an exorcism narrative at all, but the account of a conversation between Jesus and scribes from Jerusalem, who have apparently come to Galilee to see what is happening. Up this this point, Jesus has met opposition from local scribes and Pharisees, but these men from the capital would be big-wigs with considerably more authority. Whereas the controversies with the local men have centred upon Jesus' attitude to religious practice, these men are interested in the nature and source of Jesus' authority; but their objection to Jesus is presumably the same – namely the manner of his teaching, and his unconventional interpretation of the Law's demands. Since they disapprove of his teaching and his religious practice, they take exception to *all* his activity. His exorcisms, which are, as readers of the Gospel know, performed in the power of the Spirit of God, are attributed by these men to Satan: in contrast to the acknowledgment by the unclean spirit that Jesus is the Holy One of God, we have the declaration that he is possessed by Beelzebul! The activity of Jesus cannot be ignored: his extraordinary authority over demons must derive from *some* supernatural agency; and since his teaching and attitude do not agree with theirs, and since they are the guardians of the Law of God, then the logical and inevitable inference is that his power is satanic.

In reply to this charge we have three sayings of Jesus, possibly delivered by him on separate occasions, but used here together by Mark, since they are all relevant to the theme. First, the idea that Satan is warring against himself is shown to be illogical, in the parable of the divided kingdom or household: if this explanation is to be rejected, then the scribes must think again about the nature of the authority which Jesus exercises. Then the true explanation of Jesus' activity is supplied in the parable of the strong man, whose household is being plundered by someone who has bound him; this saying is perhaps a play on the name given to

Satan – Beelzebul, which means 'Lord of the house'[3] – and clearly the meaning is that the strong man Satan has been bound by someone stronger, namely Jesus, who is now plundering his household. The parable is reminiscent of Isa. 49.25, where God declares that he will take the captives from the mighty, and rescue the prey of the tyrant. The picture of the strong man being bound and plundered takes us back once more to Mark's prologue, not only to the description of the battle between Jesus and Satan, but also to John's declaration that Jesus was mightier, stronger than himself. Satan is bound, and in his expulsion of the demons Jesus is rescuing his captives and plundering his household. The final saying speaks of the sin of blasphemy against the Holy Spirit. Whatever difficulties this saying involves, the context makes quite plain how Mark understood it. Jesus spoke these words, he says, because the scribes had said: 'He has an unclean spirit.' What they *should* have said, of course, as the prologue has made clear, was: 'He has the *Holy* Spirit.' The religious leaders of Israel have seen supernatural power at work in Jesus, but instead of recognizing it as the work of God's Spirit, they have attributed it to Satan. The irony of it is, that in doing this, they have identified *themselves* with the kingdom of Satan: they see good as evil, and call truth falsehood – and *vice versa*. This is why they 'never have forgiveness', but are 'guilty of an eternal sin'. Men's reaction to the *actions* of Jesus is as critical as their reaction to his *words*; those whose hearts are hardened and whose eyes are blind are unable to see the truth, and so they call white black, and place themselves outside the kingdom.

The next passage concerning an exorcism is the story of Legion in chapter 5. In this strange story we have many of the features of a typical exorcism narrative: the plight of the sufferer is described in considerable detail, and this is followed by the spirits' recognition of Jesus, the command to them to depart, and the proof that the cure has been successful in the destruction of the pigs and the picture of the ex-demoniac clothed, seated, and in his right mind; finally we have the astonishment of the crowd when they hear of it. There are, however, several interesting features in this particular account. One is the fact that this poor man believed himself to be possessed, not by one unclean spirit, nor even by seven, but by a whole legion of them – and a Roman legion consisted of over six thousand men. As though to prove the vast number of spirits involved, Mark describes the man's colossal strength: 'No one could bind him any more, even with a chain; for he had often been bound with fetters and chains, but the chains he wrenched apart, and the fetters he broke in pieces; and no one had the strength to subdue him.' No one had the strength to subdue him because he had the strength of six thousand demons – but a few verses later we find him sitting with Jesus, clothed and in his right mind: he has met the stronger one, Jesus. Jesus has no need to bind the man himself with a chain, for he has already bound Satan, and now he has vanquished six thousand of his followers. Confronted by Jesus, the legion of unclean spirits is powerless, and demonstrates its weakness by feebly trying to adjure the Son of God in the name of God! Once again, we see the consequences of Jesus' battle with Satan: the whole satanic kingdom is crumbling.

Another strange feature of this particular story is the conversion that takes place between Jesus and the unclean spirits. The latter, apparently realizing that their time is up, admit defeat, but, anxious not to leave the neighbourhood, request that they may be allowed to enter a neighbouring herd of pigs; since these are unclean animals this would seem a suitable arrangement, but as it turns out, the move is scarcely an intelligent one, for the pigs rush into the sea and are drowned! What are we to make of this strange narrative? Did the unclean spirits suffer the same fate as the pigs, or were they merely rendered homeless once more? And why did Jesus allow the spirits to enter the pigs and destroy them? Modern readers tend to be worried by this story, and by

Jesus' apparent lack of concern for either pigs or owners. But *Jesus* is concerned with releasing a human life from the power of Satan. No doubt Mark believed that when the demons were expelled by Jesus they had to find another home – if not in the pigs, then perhaps in another human being; better that unclean animals should be destroyed than another man or woman! Probably, then, Mark supposed that the destruction of the pigs involved the destruction of their tenants – otherwise, the demons would move on and do damage elsewhere. The prophetic words of the demoniac in chapter 1 are fulfilled: Jesus has come to destroy the whole of Satan's army of unclean spirits.

When the twelve disciples are named in chapter 3, Mark tells us that Jesus appointed them 'to be with him, and to be sent out to preach, and have authority to cast out demons'. The authority Jesus gives to his disciples, like his own, links together the activities of preaching and exorcism. The same link reappears in chapter 6, where Jesus sends the disciples out, and they preach and cast out demons. In spite of their success on this mission, however, Mark's final account of an exorcism by Jesus, in chapter 9, arises out of the failure of the disciples to expel a demon. Jesus, coming down from the Mount of Transfiguration, is met with the news that the nine disciples left below had been unable to cast the demon out of a possessed child. The precise term used by Mark is one meaning that they did not have the strength – the same verb that he used in 5.4, in telling us that no one had the strength to subdue the man possessed by a legion of spirits. This time there is no conversation between the spirit and Jesus – but that is hardly surprising, since the spirit is described as dumb. The conversation on this occasion takes place between Jesus and the child's father, and is concerned with faith: Jesus, who has the faith which enables him to do all things, stands in contrast to the faithless generation with which he has to bear. It is perhaps because of the faithlessness of the present generation that spirits like this have been able to take such a hold on their victims; certainly the disciples demonstrate their lack of faith when they fail to cast out the unclean spirit, and the child's father, who doubts Jesus' ability to do so, is equally faithless. But this story is not meant to be an example of faith-healing; rather, it serves to demonstrate the vital link between the attitude to God which Mark here terms faith, and which is demonstrated in prayer, and the spiritual power which is able to defeat evil. Those who believe have their life in the kingdom, as Jesus has, and are able to grapple with Satan and defeat him; but the disciples are not yet wholly committed – like the child's father, their cry is still 'I believe; help my unbelief!'

There is one other miracle belonging in this group of exorcisms, and that is the cure of the Syrophoenician woman's daughter in chapter 7. The interest here, of course, is in the conversation with the mother – perhaps the most difficult section in the whole Gospel. Why does Jesus at first refuse to help, and then grant the woman's request? We shall perhaps find the clue to this problem if we look at the other occasion in Mark's Gospel when Jesus failed to perform a mighty work – namely in his own home town (6.1–6). In this account there is clearly a link between the refusal of the people to believe that Jesus is anything but an ordinary local boy risen above himself and his inability to do mighty works. Once again, we should not think of this connection between faith and healing simply on the level of faith-healing: what the inhabitants of Nazareth lacked – like the scribes from Jerusalem – was not the belief that Jesus had the ability to heal, but faith that the power of God was at work in him. To them, he was only the carpenter, the son of Mary. Because they fail to respond to his teaching, they cannot share in the salvation he brings: the signs of the kingdom of God are not given to those who refuse to understand their meaning. Once again, we see the link in Mark's Gospel between what Jesus says and what he does: when one is rejected, the other is withdrawn. The miracles belong within the context of the whole Gospel – and that means they are part of the proclamation of the kingdom of God. They are not wonders, to be marvelled at, but signs of God's grace.

Now in the case of the Syrophoenician, Mark has emphasized that the woman is a Gentile, and is therefore not a member of the nation of Israel, to whom the Messiah is sent. She requests a mighty work on behalf of her daughter – but since Jesus has not proclaimed the kingdom to Gentiles, she is requesting a miracle out of the context of the gospel, a mighty work detached from the kingdom itself, a crumb fallen from the table. Jesus must refuse her request: the exorcism cannot take place as it were in a vacuum, but only within the context of the advancing kingdom. But now, by her reply to Jesus, this woman acknowledges that Israel has something that the Gentiles do not have – namely, the source of nourishment; she recognizes that what she requests belongs to something greater, and shows some glimmering of understanding concerning the kingdom itself – in other words, she demonstrates true faith. And Jesus says: 'For this saying you may go your way; the demon has left your daughter.'[4]

In two of the four miracle stories that we have examined, the demons declare *who Jesus is*: they acknowledge his power and authority over them, and obey his commands. Their expulsion is part of Jesus' conquest of Satan. In the other two, the emphasis is on the attitude of those who seek help, and on their *faith in Jesus*. All these narratives are christological: the miracles are not isolated phenomena related because of their interest, but integral elements in the advancing kingdom of God, brought by Jesus. It is because they present men and women with the challenge of deciding their response to Jesus that they find a place in Mark's Gospel.

Turning now to the other group of healing miracles, we may perhaps deal with these more briefly, simply noting some of their more interesting features. First, we notice that the details of some of the stories remind us of those in the first group; the most notable example is the story of the leper (1.40–45). There is in fact no hard-and-fast line between the exorcisms and the miracles of restoration. The leprosy which made the man unclean, the fever that attacked Peter's mother-in-law (1.30f.), are regarded as personal forces which must be expelled, like the unclean spirits, if the victim is to be cured. And since these forces are hostile to God, the establishment of God's kingdom involves their overthrow. Once again, we see how Jesus' miracles are an incursion into the kingdom of Satan, which stands opposed to the rule of God. The anger and indignation which were roused in Jesus by his encounter with the leper, and which perplexed later scribes, were surely directed against Satan himself, for the leper was in his bondage, quite as much as the demoniacs. Sometimes Mark uses the word *mastix*, scourge, of disease (3.10; 5.29, 34); probably he thinks of the scourge as being in the hands of Satan. Similarly, when he speaks of a fetter which binds a man's tongue (7.35), he probably sees this as another example of Satan's handiwork. The release of men and women from bondage of any kind is part of the salvation promised in the Old Testament and now experienced in Jesus. Like Luke (4.16ff.), Mark may well have had in mind the description in Isa. 61 of one who is anointed with the Spirit of God in order to announce good tidings – the news of liberty for captives, and release for those who were bound.

Another Old Testament promise that we see being fulfilled in Mark's Gospel is Isa. 35, which describes the salvation which awaits God's people:

> Then the eyes of the blind shall be opened,
> and the ears of the deaf unstopped;
> then shall the lame man leap like a hart,
> and the tongue of the dumb sing for joy.

Mark may well have had this passage, too, in mind as he spelt out the way in which Jesus restored men and women to health; certainly the unusual word for 'dumb' (*mogilalos*) that he uses in 7.32 is found also in this passage, but nowhere else in the Greek Bible. In the healing miracles of Jesus, we see the saving activity of God himself, and Mark underlines this by using the verb 'to save' – a verb which is usually used in the Old Testament of God's salvation of his people – in the stories of Jairus' daughter, the woman with a haemorrhage and blind Bartimaeus. The miracles of restoration, no less than the exorcisms, demonstrate what we learned in the prologue: the time of salvation has arrived in the person of Jesus, in whom the renewing, creative Spirit of God is at work. For any disease which attacks a man or woman or child destroys the wholeness of life intended by God at the creation. The ears and eyes and lips which do not function, the withered hand and paralysed limbs, the lifeless body of the child and the feeble body of the woman from whom life is draining away, belong to a world where nature itself has gone astray, and is in the control of demonic forces: such things must give way before the power of God and his kingdom.

The same principle is to be seen in the nature miracles – in particular, in the stories of the stilling of the storm in chapter 4, and the walking on the water in chapter 6. The former of these again takes the form of an exorcism narrative, with Jesus addressing the wind and sea with words that he uses elsewhere in speaking to demons, and we need to remember that Mark would probably have attributed the storm to demonic powers. In the Old Testament, the sea is a frequent symbol for the powers of chaos and evil, which can be overcome only by God himself. The story ends with the awed words of the disciples: 'Who then is this, that even wind and sea obey him?' The question is left unanswered, but for readers of the Gospel there is no need of an answer; in the words of the psalm:

> Their courage melted away in their evil plight;
> they . . . were at their wits' end.

> Then they cried to the Lord in their trouble,
> and he delivered them from their distress;
> he made the storm be still,
> and the waves of the sea were hushed (Ps. 107.26–29).

Again, in the second story, when Jesus walks on the water and says 'It is I', it is possible that Mark intends us to link these words with the name of God – 'I am'. Certainly he would expect us to understand Jesus' action in walking on the water as an example of divine authority, since it was God alone who 'trampled the waves of the sea' (Job 9.8). Once again, we find that these stories, as handled by Mark, are primarily christological in their intention: they challenge us with the question posed by the disciples: 'Who then is this?'

Many commentators, however, from the early church fathers onwards, have seen a further significance in these two narratives, and interpreted them allegorically of the help brought by Christ to his persecuted church. Typical is Dennis Nineham's comment on the stilling of the storm:

> At times it might almost seem as if Christ was asleep while the Ark of his Church was being buffeted by waves of persecution and suffering; but from this story they could learn that he was in fact by no means indifferent – in response to their prayer, even if it was not accompanied by perfect faith, he would arise and deal with the forces arrayed against them.[5]

Similarly, Alan Richardson writes about the walking on the water:

> It might seem to the Christians, toiling hard at the oars against the mounting waves and contrary winds of persecution and opposition, that they were making but little headway; but at the darkest hour of the night the Lord

> would come – not as a phantom, but in His full reality, powerful to save – treading on the waves of the storm, and bringing peace.[6]

Faced with a consensus of opinion stretching from Tertullian to Nineham, it may seem foolhardy to question this interpretation! And, of course, there is no doubt that the stories were interpreted in this way from very early times: just as the parables were given allegorical interpretations, so, too, the miracle stories were applied to the situation of the early Christian communities, and interpreted symbolically. The question, however, is whether *Mark* intended the stories to be read in this way. Since there is nothing in the stories as he relates them to indicate that he meant us to give them this kind of allegorical interpretation, it would seem that Richardson has gone too far when he concludes: 'That St Mark intended this kind of interpretation to be read into his narratives seems to be beyond all reasonable doubt.' Certainly we should not allow these ideas (which were no doubt explored in many expositions of these particular stories in the early Christian assemblies) to distract from the overall impression which Mark is trying to build up of Jesus' divine authority.

A symbolic interpretation of another kind has been given to the other pair of 'nature' miracles – the two stories of the feeding of the multitudes. It may well be that these were originally variant traditions of one story, but it is clear from 8.19–21 that Mark is aware of what he is doing, and has not accidentally repeated himself. Why, then, does he include both accounts? For the popular, symbolic explanation we may turn once again to Richardson, who writes:

> In telling the two separate stories he is symbolizing the offering of salvation 'to the Jew first, but also to the Greek' . . . From the time of St Augustine the suggestion has been known that the Feeding of the Five Thousand

> represents Christ's communication of Himself to the Jews, and that of the Four Thousand represents His self-communication to the Gentiles. The disciples need have no anxiety concerning Christ's ability to supply spiritual food to the whole Gentile world.[7]

In support of this interpretation Richardson argues that the crowd fed in chapter 8 were probably thought by Mark to be Gentile, because the last place to be mentioned was the district of Decapolis in 7.31; maintains that the fact that Mark uses two different words for 'basket' (the first of which is distinctively Jewish) on the two different occasions; and suggests that the numbers involved in the two stories are significant. The five loaves fed to the five thousand are said to symbolize the five books of the Law, while the twelve baskets left over symbolize the twelve tribes of Israel. The seven loaves fed to the four thousand and the seven baskets left over could represent either the seven deacons in Acts 6 or the seventy nations of the Jewish world. Richardson concludes:

> In view of this wealth of accumulative evidence it is impossible to doubt that St Mark intended his readers to understand the interpretation of the feeding miracles which has been suggested above.

Once again, however, Richardson has more than overstated his case. To the 'wealth' of his evidence we may reply: first, that Mark's geographical references are vague, and that it is by no means certain that the four thousand, some of whom have come a long way, are in fact Gentiles; if this is the point of the second story, Mark's failure to make the point clear is quite extraordinary. Secondly, that though Mark does apparently distinguish between the two words for 'basket', this may well be due to his sources; moreover, though one term may refer to a type of basket used only among Jews, this does not mean that the second, more general word indicates a basket used only by Gentiles. Thirdly, that something very serious is wrong with the arithmetic. Five loaves for the Pentateuch is understandable (though one hardly expects to find Mark suggesting that Jesus feeds the crowds with the Jewish Law!), but one might expect the twelve tribes of Israel to be symbolized by the number in the crowd (perhaps twelve thousand) rather than by the surplus basketfuls. Even more problems arise in the second story: how can seven be said to equal seventy? And why should four thousand people be fed?

This kind of interpretation reflects an imagination which has been allowed to run riot; no doubt the stories were interpreted in this way from an early date, but if Mark had intended us to understand them as feedings of Jews and Gentiles, he would surely have given us bigger and better clues. As it is, his summary of the two stories in chapter 8 suggests that he believes that the meaning of these two accounts stares us in the face. What, then, is their meaning? There are points of contact between these two narratives and the account of the Last Supper in chapter 14 which suggest that Mark, like John (in John 6), had in mind the spiritual significance of the feeding. But both stories centre on the satisfaction of physical hunger, and that must be their primary significance. The provision of food in the desert for those who are hungry inevitably reminds us of the way in which, in the past, as part of the salvation which took place at the Exodus, God had fed his people with manna in the wilderness. The picture of one whom we know to be the Messiah feeding his people ought to point us also to the great messianic feast which lay in the future. These two ideas of course belong together, for what happened at the Exodus was seen by the Hebrew prophets as the pattern for the salvation of God which lay in the future, and sometimes this hope was expressed in terms of being fed once again by God: 'On this mountain,' declared Isaiah, 'the Lord of hosts will make for all peoples a feast of fat things, of fat things full of marrow' (Isa. 25.6). Later, we find the rabbis drawing a parallel between Moses and the Messiah: 'As the first redeemer caused manna to descend, so shall also the last redeemer cause manna to descend.' If these are the clues to Mark's understanding of the feeding stories, they suggest that these miracles, like all the others, are seen by Mark as indications that the time of salvation announced in the prologue has arrived. The feeding of the people, like their healing, is a sign of the wholeness of life which is found in the kingdom.

Mark clearly considered these two feeding miracles to be particularly important and significant. Perhaps this is why he includes both accounts. When in 6.52 he describes the terror of the disciples at seeing Jesus walking on the water, he explains it by saying: 'They were utterly astounded, for they did not understand about the loaves, but their hearts were hardened.' Mark obviously believed that if the disciples *had* understood the significance of the loaves, they would have understood also that Jesus had power over the wind and the waves: if they had realized why and how Jesus was able to feed the people, they would have expected him to be able to control the elements. A similar interpretation is given in chapter 8, but this time it is found in the mouth of Jesus himself. Following the account of the second feeding we have the request of the Pharisees for a sign. How absurd their request seems in such a context! They fail to see what is there to be seen; naturally Jesus refuses their demand. This leads into a discussion between Jesus and his disciples in a boat, in which Jesus warns the disciples: 'Take heed, beware of the leaven of the Pharisees and the leaven of Herod,' while they, with what seems incredible stupidity, discuss the fact that they have brought no bread with them. Possibly Mark has at this point inserted an isolated saying of Jesus into the conversation about bread, for the warning against leaven seems to interrupt the rest of the paragraph.

But why should he place the saying at this point? Professor Nineham, in his commentary, suggests that Mark incorporated it here 'because the reference to bread in v. 14 provided as good a context for it as he could find'.[8] But did Mark not see any closer link than this between Jesus' words and the rest of the conversation? And why did he think the disciples needed to be warned against the Pharisees' leaven? The two questions answer each other, for what the Pharisees and the disciples share in common in Mark's view, to greater or lesser degree, is obtuseness,[9] a lack of understanding which renders them incapable of comprehending the evidence which is placed before them. The Pharisees have seen Jesus heal men's bodies and exorcize demons, and yet they demand a sign; the disciples have twice seen Jesus feed vast numbers of people, and yet they are worried because they have forgotten to bring bread. The same hardness of heart has been demonstrated by Herod in his treatment of John. What, then, is the leaven of the Pharisees and of Herod? In rabbinic writings, as in the New Testament, leaven is usually used of an evil tendency in man which pervades and corrupts him altogether. Matthew's version of this saying interprets it of teaching, Luke's as hypocrisy, while modern commentators take the words as a warning against the false piety of the Pharisees and the godlessness of the Herodians or the hostility of them both. None of these suggestions, however, has much relevance to the context in which Mark has set the saying. I suggest that he understood 'leaven' as that rigid attitude which affects the whole personality, making men self-righteous, uncomprehending and hard-hearted, so that they are unable to see the evidence that is placed before them, or to accept the truth when it is presented to them. This influence has completely pervaded the leaders of the nation, and the disciples, by their complete failure to understand the significance of the healing miracles, show that they are in danger, as Jesus suggests, of being equally blind to the truth.

In the ensuing conversation, we are reminded of the details of the two feedings. Are the numbers significant in themselves? And why is the miracle repeated? Are we to think of Jews and Gentiles being fed, as so many commentators argue – or is it perhaps simply that since Israel was fed again and again in the wilderness, Jesus does the same now? The numbers of people and loaves involved underline the significance of what takes place, while the insistence on the large quantities of food left over on both occasions demonstrates the superiority of what is taking place now, through Jesus, to what took place at the Exodus – for the distinctive feature of manna was that it could *not* be left over, but had to be consumed at once. But what was to happen to the broken fragments? This, surely, is where the Gentiles come in. Moses fed Israel in the wilderness, and now Israel is fed again by her Messiah, but in the story of the Syrophoenician woman Mark has already shown us that while the children are fed first, even Gentiles may gather up the crumbs that fall. In the gathering up of the broken fragments, we see hints of the future mission of the disciples to the Gentiles; Jesus himself may be able to preach only to Israel, but his followers will take the gospel to the world.

FOUR

The Secret

We have looked at the way in which Mark lays his cards on the table in his opening paragraphs. On the very first page, he told us clearly who Jesus is: the Christ, the one expected by the prophets, the mighty one foretold by John, the one anointed with the Spirit, the Son of God who does battle with Satan. From there on, we have watched Jesus doing precisely the kind of things we would expect: we have seen him routing the forces of Satan – throwing out demons, healing men and women with diseases, subduing the wind and the waves, providing food for the people; we have seen him preaching good news, and teaching with authority. But though it is clear to us, reading Mark's Gospel, that Jesus does these things because he is who he is, everyone in the story is left asking: How does he do it? What is going on? Who is he? Because they have not read Mark's prologue, they do not understand what is happening.

So we come to the theme of the secret. Our problem is not simply that the characters in the story do not understand what is happening, but that the secret seems – at least in part – to be deliberate. Jesus' identity is deliberately concealed from men and women. Why?

Reading through Mark's Gospel, there are certain scenes that stand out; they are significant not simply in themselves, but as important turning points in the narrative. The most obvious example is the story of Caesarea Philippi, at the end of chapter 8, which has often been described as the 'watershed' of the Gospel. Whether Mark himself is responsible for making the story play this crucial role is difficult to say.

It used to be assumed, of course, that the incident was by its very nature a turning-point; that it must have had the same function in the life of Jesus as in the Gospel of Mark. Leaving aside altogether the question of what exactly happened at Caesarea Philippi, it is clear that this is by no means necessarily so. The reason that this incident is a turning point in the narrative is at least partly due to the arrangement of the material on either side of it. And it is not only the material immediately before and after that is important here. The whole direction of the Gospel changes at this point. Before this conversation between Jesus and his disciples, Jesus teaches the crowds and performs miracles. After it, he teaches his disciples and performs only one or two miracles, to which Mark attaches symbolic meaning. Caesarea Philippi marks the beginning of the journey to the cross. Clearly Mark sees it as a significant happening; but what does he understand by it? What causes confusion and makes the whole scene enigmatic is the command to silence which follows Peter's so-called confession. This has been interpreted in at least three different ways. At one end of the spectrum, it has been taken to mean: 'Yes, you are right; but do not tell anyone.' This seems to be how Matthew understood it. At the other, it has been interpreted as a repudiation of the title of Messiah. And in between, it has been understood as a qualified acceptance of the role of Messiah, even though that particular term is inadequate.

How, then, did Mark understand the words that he attributes to Jesus here? This is a complex problem, but let me say straight away that I am totally unpersuaded by the arguments of those who maintain that Mark intended to portray Jesus as firmly *rejecting* the title of Messiah.[1] If *this* is what Mark is trying to say, then one can only conclude that he is very bad indeed at saying it! Certainly Matthew, who is perhaps Mark's earliest interpreter, did not understand the scene in that way, for he added Jesus' commendation of Peter: the declaration that Jesus is the Christ cannot be wrong, for it is an insight given to him by God. We ought also to compare the conversation which Mark describes as taking place while Jesus and three of his disciples were coming down from the Mount of Transfiguration. Once again, Jesus enjoined secrecy about what had taken place. Are we to conclude that Mark thinks of Jesus as repudiating what had happened on the mountain? Of course not! On this occasion, the confession of Jesus' identity has come from heaven itself: clearly we may accept God's own testimony to his Son as correct! The command to silence in 9.9, then, certainly cannot be seen as a rejection of what has just taken place.

The choice, then, as far as our understanding of Mark's portrayal of the scene is concerned, seems to be between seeing Jesus' words as meaning 'Yes – but this is not the time to proclaim my messiahship' or 'Yes – but this is not the best way of putting it' or 'Yes – but this is something that can be understood only by those who are my disciples.' In which of these ways does he mean us to understand it?

In asking the question 'How does Mark understand the command to secrecy?' we are raising a question which concerns far more than this one story. There are in Mark several occasions where Jesus apparently imposes silence on his disciples, or on those whom he has healed, about what they have experienced. It was William Wrede who first raised the problem of the messianic secret in Mark, and who suggested that the motif of secrecy is primarily a theological idea.[2] And it has to be admitted that there is something artificial about some of these commands to secrecy. Whether or not any of them go back to Jesus is not our concern here; we are concerned with Mark's interpretation of the story, and with the truth that he is trying to convey to his readers. Whatever else it may or may not be, for Mark the theme of secrecy is a theological motif: he uses it to tell us something about Jesus – and about the way in which men and women reacted to him. Let us look, then, at the evidence.

The starting point of our enquiry is the story of Caesarea Philippi. It is worth noting that the so-called confession of Peter is set in the context of a double enquiry from Jesus. His first question concerns the beliefs that 'men' hold about him; then, in contrast, he asks: 'But you, what do *you* say about me?' The division that is made at Caesarea Philippi is not, in Mark, a division between what the disciples believed about Jesus beforehand and what they believed afterwards. Rather, it is a division between non-believers and believers, between outsiders and disciples, between those who are blind to the significance of Jesus and those whose eyes have been opened. The crowd, who have seen Jesus' miracles and heard him teach, have responded with amazement, but with lack of comprehension; his mighty works and words suggest that he is a man of God – he must, they think, be John the Baptist back from the dead, or Elijah, or one of the other prophets. Those same suggestions have been made before; the summary in 8.28 echoes the words of the people and the judgment of King Herod in 6.14ff. This is the response of outsiders to Jesus, the worker of miracles. In contrast, Peter declares his belief that Jesus is the Christ. The natural way of interpreting this scene is to conclude that the people have got Jesus wrong, and the disciples have grasped at least something of the truth. If Mark is indeed rejecting a false christology, as some commentators seem now to suppose, then this false view of Jesus is attributed to the crowd, not to the disciples. It is the crowd who are astonished at what Jesus does, and who think of him as a wonder-worker. The confession of Jesus as the Christ may be inadequate, but it is at least a platform on which Jesus can begin to teach his disciples the true meaning of his messiahship. If it is Peter who then proves unable to comprehend this teaching, this is because he is like the blind man in the story that immediately precedes this one – his eyes have been partly opened, but he certainly cannot be said to see clearly; to him, men and trees look alike.

The scene at Caesarea Philippi is thus a story of seeing and partly seeing. The evidence has been there for all to see. Those outside are totally blind to the true significance of Jesus. Those who are his disciples have been given insight – but still grasp only part of the truth; to them Jesus must give special teaching in private. Even this – to mix the metaphors – falls on deaf ears. Nevertheless, it is the confession that Jesus is the Christ that marks these men out. They have at least begun to grasp the truth.

The interesting thing about this pattern is that it is by no means unique to this particular story. We tend to put the story of Caesarea Philippi in a special category, of course, but perhaps in doing so we miss the similarity with other stories in the Gospel. Let us look again, for example, at what happens in chapter 4. Here, Jesus teaches a large crowd; they all have the opportunity of hearing his teaching. What he teaches them – the parable of the Sower – is itself a parable about the way in which his hearers respond to his teaching. The great majority of them listen eagerly to what he has to say, but their response is only temporary – it has no depth to it: they marvel at his words, but they do not really hear what he has to say; a few, however, respond to his words and produce fruit. Mark follows the parable with an allegorical interpretation, showing how he understood it. The contrast is between those who hear the word but – sooner or later – reject it, and those who hear it and accept it. In the parable there are, of course, four groups: there are those who hear the word but who never accept it, because Satan prevents them; there are those who do respond – but who cannot accept the suffering that comes to them on account of the word, and who therefore fall away; there are those who hear the word but who are soon distracted; and finally, there are those who have ears to hear – who hear the word, receive it, and bear fruit. Yet for Mark, as we have already seen, there are really only two groups: there are those who hear the word and those who do not. In between the parable and its interpretation Mark has slipped three vital verses: 'To you,' says Jesus, 'has been given the secret of the kingdom of God, but for those outside everything is in parables.' The explanation of the parable is given in private to the Twelve and those who were about him. The same teaching has been given to everyone, but for the great majority of Jesus' hearers, his teaching remains *en parabolais* – and that Greek phrase can mean not only 'in parables', but also 'in riddles'; perhaps that is its meaning here, for certainly Mark means that they do not understand. The disciples do not understand either, but at least they have sufficient insight to realize that they do not understand, sufficient faith to come to Jesus and ask for an explanation. To them is given the secret of the kingdom of God. The important division, then, is between those who are with Jesus and those who are outside; between those who see and hear all that he does, but do not perceive its true significance, and those who are prepared to look for the meaning of what he is doing and saying.

Now there is clearly a secret here – indeed, most of our English versions use the word 'secret'. But it is not so much a question of the secret being hidden as of its being revealed. Jesus has taught the word openly, and the way in which the explanation of the parable is introduced in v. 13 suggests that its meaning should have been clear without any further instruction. The secret is not deliberately hidden – it is there, for anyone with eyes to see and ears to hear. There is no contradiction, then, between what is said here and Mark's summary at the end of the chapter, in vv. 33f.: 'With many such parables he spoke the word to them, as they were able to hear it. He did not speak to them without a parable, but privately to his own disciples he explained everything.' Contrary to what is sometimes suggested, Mark does *not* think of the parables as intended to mystify Jesus' hearers. Their meaning may not be immediately obvious, but they are a challenge, and they call for a response. To those who are prepared to respond, understanding will be given.

I have suggested that this scene in Mark 4, where Jesus teaches the people openly and the disciples secretly, is similar to that in chapter 8, where the disciples acknowledge Jesus as Messiah. Now of course, it is easy to point out differences in the stories. In Mark 4, the secret that is revealed is the secret about the kingdom of God, while in Mark 8 it is the secret of Jesus' own identity; the difference may be more apparent than real, since it is clear that for Mark Jesus and the kingdom of God are tied up together. The 'word' that Jesus proclaims is the arrival of the kingdom, but the all-important division which takes place in chapter 4 is essentially the result of the response which men and women make to the person of Jesus. A second difference between the stories is that in chapter 4 there is no command to secrecy. The secret of the kingdom is hidden from outsiders – but not deliberately. It is available to those who are prepared to accept it. The emphasis in this scene is on the fact that what is hidden to outsiders is revealed to disciples. Nevertheless, the basic contrasts between outsiders and disciples, between what is hidden and what is revealed, between incomprehension and understanding, is the same. Indeed, we might perhaps take these two scenes in Mark as paradigms for two related themes which are found throughout his Gospel. For if we talk about a messianic secret, we ought also to talk about revelation; the theme of disclosure is quite as important for Mark as that of concealment. But let us look first at other commands to secrecy.

They fall into two groups. The first group may properly be described as part of the messianic secret, for they are concerned with Jesus' identity. Perhaps the clearest example, apart from 8.30, is 3.11f. Here unclean spirits acknowledge Jesus with the words 'You are the Son of God', and he commands them not to make him known – the injunction is worded very closely to that in 8.30. Perhaps we should include also 1.25, since that follows a similar confession by an unclean spirit: 'I know who you are – the Holy One of God'; but the statement that Jesus silenced him is a natural one in the context, and it is not clear that Mark meant to imply any more than the fact that Jesus brought the spirit under control. Strictly speaking, the only three texts which fall into this group are 3.12; 8.30 and 9.9.

By contrast, there are three texts where the identity of Jesus is proclaimed, and where no attempt is made to conceal what is said. The placing of these three passages, however, and their character, is significant. The first occurs in 1.11 – the words addressed to Jesus from heaven at his baptism: 'You are my beloved Son, in you I am well pleased.' There is no need for any command to secrecy here, however, for in Mark's scene it is only Jesus who hears the words. They are addressed to him, not to the crowds, nor to John the Baptist, and the only other people to 'hear' the words are the readers of the Gospel. But they, of course, are followers of Jesus, to whom this 'secret' has already been revealed. We have seen already that the whole of this introductory section of Mark is a spelling-out of the truth about Jesus which is 'hidden' throughout most of the Gospel.

The other two texts occur at the very end of the Gospel. The first is Mark 14.62, where Jesus declares 'I am'. These words are of course an answer to the question put by the high priest: 'Are you the Christ, the Son of the Beloved?' Whether or not any such question was ever put in this form is another of those historical questions which, fortunately, we do not have to solve in asking questions about Mark. The significant fact in considering Mark's presentation is that at this point the 'messianic secret' is out. And why not? Jesus does not proclaim himself as Messiah; he will not allow his disciples to proclaim him. But if others see what he does and hears his words and draw the right conclusion, why should he deny it – if he *is* the Christ? And if those others should be represented by the high priest of Israel, what could be more appropriate? The irony of the scene is, of course, that the high priest is very far from seeing or hearing or understanding the truth. His words come from 'hardness of heart' – the refusal to believe – not from faith; his only purpose is to find some grounds on which to condemn Jesus to death. The reply of Jesus as given in Mark is clear and unambiguous.[3] At this point Jesus acknowledges himself to be what we, the readers of the Gospel, have known him to be since page 1.[4]

The final passage is 15.39. At the moment of Jesus' death, the Roman centurion responsible for his death acknowledges as Son of God. No matter that the phrase lacks the definite article; no matter that the Roman centurion certainly could not have meant what Christians mean by 'Son of God', even if he uttered the phrase. Here is an open confession of Jesus. And it is made at the moment of Jesus' death.

It is interesting to notice how few texts there are, in Mark, which deal specifically with the messiahship of Jesus, either to affirm it or deny it – and by 'messiahship' I mean an understanding of the mission of Jesus described in a variety of terms or titles, not just the word 'Messiah'. It is not Mark's way to spell out the identity of Jesus – in the way that the author of John's Gospel does later. But, of course, the material that Mark presents is in his view blatantly messianic. Throughout the early chapters of the Gospel, we watch Jesus acting in a variety of ways with authority – teaching, healing, commanding men to follow him, challenging the religious authorities and so on. 'What is this?' ask the people. There has to be an explanation of this authority – and we have seen already that two rival ones are presented in chapter 3: Jesus is acting either with the authority of Satan, or with that of the Holy Spirit. At the end of chapter 4, the first of a series of miracle stories leaves the disciples asking the question 'Who is this?' The miracles that follow spell out the answer, for those with eyes to see and ears to hear. Yet in 8.11–13, immediately after the feeding of four thousand men, the Pharisees come to him and demand a sign! In view of all that Jesus has done, their request is absurd. They ask for proof, and demand credentials. But what Jesus is cannot be separated from the things that he does and proclaims.

And at the end of the Gospel, Jesus is proclaimed king by the crowds as he enters Jerusalem, anointed king by a woman, and acts with extraordinary authority in the temple; he even teaches by means of a parable in which he refers to himself as 'beloved Son'. Yet it is all lost on his contemporaries. Only a few individuals (like blind Bartimaeus on the road outside Jericho) grasp something of the truth. The secret is proclaimed – but the proclamation is hidden. The two ideas, of manifestation and secrecy, belong together.

There is, however, a second group of passages where we meet the idea of secrecy. These are miracle stories. Sometimes we find Jesus enjoining secrecy on those whom he has healed. The strangest is 5.43, where witnesses are told to keep silent about the raising of Jairus' daughter. How could such an event be kept secret? The leper in 1.44 is told to go straight to the priest without saying anything; that might be no more than a command for speed in fulfilling the Law's requirements, but Mark stresses the disobedience of the healed man, who could not keep quiet. The command to say nothing occurs also in 7.36 and 8.26, where a deaf man and a blind man are healed.

Now in the last two cases, we shall not be surprised if Mark uses the restoration of a deaf man and a blind man as symbols of belief in Jesus. Indeed, in the latter case, he has quite clearly used the blind man in this way. Does he mean us to see the command to the healed man in 8.26 to keep what has happened private, as parallel to the command to the disciples in 8.30? And is the command to the deaf man in 7.36 also a reminder that those who have had their ears opened understand something which cannot be grasped by those who have not been given faith, however much the word may be proclaimed? It is no good telling people who Jesus is if they are blind and deaf to the truth. In the case of Jairus' daughter, we certainly have something which cannot be understood except by those who believe in the power of Jesus, himself raised from the dead, to give life to others. Perhaps behind all these commands to secrecy in Mark (and that includes the command to the leper in 1.44) there lies the conviction that the miracles of Jesus *cannot* be understood except by those who believe in Jesus as the Son of God. To proclaim the miracles apart from that context of faith is to proclaim them simply as mighty wonders – the kind of signs the Pharisees demanded – and not as examples of his saving power. The secrecy, then is a symbol of unbelief. The identity of Jesus is hidden from those who do not believe.

This interpretation seems to be confirmed if we look at those stories where, by contrast, there is *no* element of secrecy. In chapter 5 we have two; the demoniac, healed of a legion of unclean spirits, is told to go and tell his people what the Lord has done for him. It is worth noting that Jesus tells him that his faith has healed him, and that the man wishes to follow him as a disciple: those who believe may proclaim what the Lord has done for them. In the story that follows, in 5.30, the woman with a haemorrhage *tries* to keep things secret but is dragged out into the open by Jesus; healing cannot be had on the quiet – as a magical rite; it needs open confession of her faith in Jesus' power to heal her; and it is her faith, says Jesus, that has healed her. It is worth comparing the story of the Syrophoenician woman in 7.24–30, who demonstrates her faith in Jesus, and so has her request granted. Although the woman and her child did not belong to Israel, and so were outside the scope of God's promises and Jesus' ministry, they were allowed to share in the gifts of the kingdom. Miracles are not crumbs, to be thrown to all and sundry, but have to be received in the context of faith. This is why Jesus was unable, Mark tells us, to do any mighty works in his own town (6.1–6).

Finally, we have a rather different command for silence. The blind man outside Jericho who appeals to Jesus for help and addresses him as 'Son of David', is told to keep quiet, not by Jesus, but by the crowd (10.46–52). The man's faith may be inadequate, but Jesus does not rebuke him, or tell him he has used the wrong title; on the contrary, he heals the man, telling him that his faith has saved him – and he follows Jesus on the way to Jerusalem. As for the crowd, they do not 'hear' what the man says, for they do not believe.

These, then, are the various ways in which Mark uses the theme of the secret. What conclusions are we to draw?

First of all, it is clear that the secret is concerned with who Jesus is. We see this, for example, in the story of Caesarea Philippi, where Jesus asks his disciples, 'Who do you say that I am?', and in the story of the transfiguration in the next chapter, where the voice from heaven declares: 'This is my beloved Son.' If the secret is linked with miracles and parables, as well as with straightforward declarations of Jesus' identity, it is because they, too, reveal who he is.

Secondly, the secret is tied up with faith in Jesus. Only those who believe in him understand who he is. Simply seeing and hearing the words and deeds of Jesus do not necessarily persuade men and women of the truth. Outsiders look at the evidence and fail to comprehend what it means. It requires a personal commitment to Jesus to recognize that God is working through him.

Much of the tension in maintaining the secret in Mark's Gospel is due to his method in telling the story. Because both he and his readers share faith in Jesus, he is able to tell the story at two levels. There is the 'earthly' level of comprehension – or rather, of incomprehension! And there is a 'spiritual' level, where the truth is known. Every now and then Mark pulls back the shutters from this second level, and allows his readers to see scenes (for example the transfiguration) which remind us of the truths spelt out in the prologue.

Finally, the secret *remains* secret (more or less) till the very end of the story. Only at the resurrection do men and women really grasp the truth. Throughout his ministry, the disciples are pictured as being only half aware of the truth. Mysteriously, it is through his death that Jesus is crowned as king, and through his resurrection that men's eyes are finally opened.

How, then, did Mark understand Jesus' response to Peter at Caesarea Philippi? It looks very much as though he would have agreed with two of my suggestions. Clearly, the words of Jesus can be understood to mean: 'Yes, I am the Messiah – but this is not the time to proclaim my messiahship, for it will only be after the resurrection that this can be understood.' Equally, they can be understood to mean: 'Yes, I am the Messiah – but this is something that can be understood only by my disciples; those who do not have faith in me cannot comprehend it? But what of the third suggestion – the way in which these words are so often understood? Can they mean: 'Yes, I am the Messiah – but that is not the best way of putting it. It is better to speak of me in other terms'? This must be the theme of our next chapter.

FIVE

What's in a Name?

In the last chapter we explored the way in which Mark makes use of the idea of the secret to explain why it was that the truth about Jesus was grasped only after the resurrection. One of the puzzling things about this secret is that though it is clear that what is hidden is Jesus' true identity, there seem to be many different ways of expressing it. Although scholars tend to talk about the 'messianic' secret, Mark apparently regarded not only the term 'Messiah' (or 'Christ'), but also 'Son of God', 'Holy One of God' and 'King of the Jews' as true descriptions of Jesus. In addition, there is the enigmatic 'title' used by Jesus himself – 'the Son of man' – which is *not* part of the secret in Mark's scheme, even though its meaning is for twentieth-century readers the greatest mystery of all.

One of our difficulties in trying to comprehend Mark is that we tend to assume that all these terms were ready-made titles when Mark used them, with clear, well-defined meanings. In fact, however, in Mark's time they were more general than precise – it would be better to term them 'descriptions' rather than 'titles' – and the meaning that each now has is very largely the result of its association with the figure of Jesus. We may compare what happens in the traditional story of Prince Charming searching for his princess. The picture of the princess is vague: we know simply that she will be worthy of the prince and of the fame and fortune that await her. Usually, indeed, the story proves to have a twist; the princess is *not* what we might expect, but is found in the most unlikely quarter, a humble peasant girl rather than the daughter of a king. But once the prince's hoped-for bride is discovered, she is identified as *the* Princess: now she is discovered to have all the qualities that we expected – beauty, grace, gentleness, charm. Once she is identified, it becomes obvious to all the Prince's loyal subjects that this was precisely the girl they were looking for all along. From now on, when anyone refers to 'the Princess', they will be thinking of this particular girl, and those who were once regarded as candidates will be forgotten. So the experience shapes the title – indeed, it turns what was previously only a general description (a princess) into a title (*the* Princess).

Many of the terms applied to Jesus are like this; the meaning that attaches to them in our minds is the result of their application to Jesus, and they have become titles through being used of him. The term 'Messiah', for example, was originally an adjective meaning 'anointed', and was used in Judaism of a variety of gifted people – 'anointed' by God's Spirit for some particular task – so that to say that Jesus was 'Messiah' was not nearly as narrow a definition as we today assume. But once the term was applied to Jesus, he became for Christians the *only* Messiah. From now on, Jesus was the Messiah and the Messiah was Jesus. A further development took place when the term was translated into Greek as 'Christ'. Now its true meaning was forgotten, and it became little more than a proper name. The only form of anointing with which the Greek world was familiar was part of the ritual of taking a bath, so that to preach Jesus as 'the anointed one' might well have caused some puzzlement! Clearly, it was meaningless for Gentiles with no Jewish background to be asked to believe that Jesus was 'the Christ' or 'anointed one'; but to use the strange Hebrew term 'Messiah' would be equally obscure – the equivalent of proclaiming that Jesus was 'the Mahdi' to a group of Englishmen.[1] New ways had to be sought to express faith in Jesus, as the gospel was taken beyond the confines of Judaism.

But even before words lost their meaning by being transferred from one culture to another in this way, it seems that no one term was ever adequate to express what Christians believed about Jesus. Just as our young Prince Charming seizes on every appropriate noun and adjective he can call to mind in order to try to describe the object of his love, so the early Christians took up every term expressing Jewish hopes and longings, and applied them to Jesus. The various descriptions were in no way exclusive – it was not a case of believing *either* that Jesus was 'Son of God' *or* that he was 'Lord'; like photographs taken from different angles, each term expressed something of the truth. It has sometimes been argued that there were different 'christologies', each with its own 'title', in different Christian communities, but while it is true that one term may have been more meaningful to one group than to another, there is no reason why they should have been seen as alternatives. It is more likely that they were all treated as grist to the mill. In the same way, the eighteenth-century hymn-writer John Newton attempted to sum up what Jesus meant to him:

> Jesus, my Shepherd, Brother, Friend,
> My Prophet, Priest, and King,
> My Lord, my Life, my Way, my End,
> Accept the praise I bring.

Yet it is clear that even if *all* these titles are added together, they still cannot represent the whole truth. Each of them is an image, used in an attempt to express something which is inexpressible, and even if we put them all together, we still have only a collection of pictorial images, not a definitive statement about who Jesus 'is'.

Conventional studies of New Testament christology have often proceeded by examining each of the 'titles' of Jesus in turn. For various reasons, however, this may be a misleading approach. First of all, we have seen in previous chapters that there are other ways of expressing belief about Jesus: 'titles' may be convenient ways of summing up beliefs, but they are only part of the picture. Secondly, many of the 'titles' have changed their meaning over the centuries, as they have moved from one context to another and changed their associations. We have seen already how 'Messiah', a term so full of meaning among Jews, was without any content at all outside Judaism. Something rather different happened with the phrase 'the Son of God'. Like the term 'Messiah', this phrase seems to have been more widely used among Jews than we tend to imagine. It was an appropriate description of the relationship between God and his people – a relationship involving election, obedience, and mutual love. So Israel is called 'God's Son' (Hos. 11.1), as is their representative, the king (Ps. 2.7), and those who are 'righteous' or faithful to God (Wisdom 2.18; 5.5). Clearly it was an appropriate term to use of God's expected Messiah. But it is also clear that when the gospel was preached to Gentiles, this particular term would have been understood rather differently: 'Son of God' was not a strange term for them, unlike 'Messiah', but was familiar enough, for 'the sons of the gods' were divine beings, and so the phrase would have been heard and understood in that way. This change in meaning was not the end of the story, however, for 'Son of God' became in time one of the key affirmations of the Christian creeds, and was interpreted as a way of expressing Christ's divine nature. This makes it difficult for Christians of the twentieth century to understand the phrase in the way that Mark understood it; influenced by more than nineteen centuries of Christian tradition, we inevitably read the words in the light of our own experience and beliefs.

There is a third reason why concentration on the 'titles' of Jesus can be misleading. This is because, as we have seen already, many of them were originally not titles at all! Most of them would be better termed descriptive phrases, which have *become* titles through being used of Jesus. Once again we may think of our Prince Charming, trying adequately to describe the object of his love. She is his 'Beloved', the one perfect 'Rose' of his dreams, an 'Angel', his 'Sweetheart'. The terms he uses are not in themselves titles; in other contexts they could be used in different ways of a variety of people, but in this context their meaning is narrowed down by being applied to one particular person. We have looked already at the way in which the adjective 'Messiah' became a title when the idea of God's anointed was narrowed down to one particular individual. The important question for us is, of course, did this happen *before* the time of Jesus, or did it come about as a result of faith that Jesus was the one who was truly God's anointed? The answer may well be that the development involved both processes: that already, before the time of Jesus, the idea of 'God's anointed' was being focussed on a future figure, but that when it was first used of Jesus it was still a description, rather than a title.

By the time we come to Mark, of course, we may perhaps fairly describe these terms as 'titles'. But we shall certainly misunderstand what was happening if we think that there was a kind of ready-made 'list' of 'messianic titles', and that the early Christians went down this list ticking them off one by one! Surprisingly, those terms which we would put on such a list – 'Son of God', 'Son of man', 'Suffering Servant', 'Lord', even 'Messiah' – were not ready-made titles at all. The difference can perhaps be illustrated if we think, on the one hand, of a chef carefully preparing a meal for a special occasion, knowing exactly what each course is to be, and what ingredients are required, and on the other, of what happens when those of us who are less well-organized wander into the kitchen, inspect the contents of the refrigerator, and wonder how we can best use the ingredients available to make a reasonably appetizing meal. In the one case, there are ready-made ideas in the mind of the cook (Boeuf à la Mode, Oeufs à la Neige . . .) and the reality conforms (in the hands of an expert) to the expectation; in the other, the expectation is less specific, and we use whatever materials happen to be available. In christology, we tend to assume that in the earliest stages of Christian belief, the categories used by preachers were part of a previously drawn-up 'job description', and that the difficulty of finding appropriate terms to use of Jesus is a problem of translation that arises when the gospel is taken from one culture to another. We can understand why the Eskimo should be baffled by the statement that Jesus is the Good Shepherd, and we can see that most of the world is likely to look blank when informed that Jesus is the Messiah, since they understand neither the name 'Jesus' nor the term 'Messiah'. The missionary preacher today needs first of all to give some kind of picture of Jesus, and he will then try to find appropriate ways of expressing the significance that Jesus has for Christian believers. We need to realize, however, that the problem existed also for the earliest Christian preachers: first-century Jews did not have the clear expectations of a future redeemer which we suppose they had – rather, they had a jumble of hopes and longings much closer to the vague though possibly grandiose ideas that I have when I survey my refrigerator shelves than to the clearly articulated plans of the professional chef. We must therefore think of these early preachers searching for ways of describing their new experience, rather than *expecting* particular experiences and finding them realized in Jesus. Naturally they turned to the Old Testament in trying to find appropriate terms to express their faith: every hope and longing set out there was more than fulfilled in Jesus, and every term which expressed God's promises could be applied to him. It is in the writings of Paul and John especially that we see this great variety of Old Testament imagery being plundered in the interests of christology.

There is one particular term which causes tremendous difficulties for us today, and this is the phrase 'the Son of man'. One of the intriguing things about the way this term is used is that Mark apparently did not regard it as part of the 'secret' about Jesus. According to Mark, the phrase was used frequently by Jesus himself, usually in speaking to his disciples, but also openly in talking to outsiders and opponents. Thus we have the interesting parallel in the use of 'titles' between the scene with his disciples at Caesarea Philippi and the trial of Jesus by his enemies: in both cases, Jesus substitutes the phrase 'the Son of man' for the term 'the Messiah', which has been used by Peter and by the high priest. This picture of Jesus speaking freely of himself as 'the Son of man' tallies with the fact that there is no evidence that this term was used by early Christians to express their faith in Jesus; with the sole exception of Acts 7.56, the phrase is found only in the mouth of Jesus himself. As far as we know, Christians never declared that 'Jesus is the Son of man', in the way that they confessed 'Jesus is the Messiah', or 'Jesus is Lord' or 'Jesus is the Son of God'. From Mark's point of view, therefore, the term was not part of the 'secret' about Jesus which was given only to those with faith to grasp his true identity. He seems to have regarded the phrase as Jesus' own enigmatic way of speaking about himself, rather than as some open claim to messianic status. Now it has often been assumed that 'the Son of man' was a well-known messianic 'title' in first century Judaism, and that Jesus himself was claiming to *be* 'the Son of man'. If this were so, we should have to explain why his followers failed to acknowledge him by the title which he himself had claimed: it would be strange indeed if the one 'title' which Jesus had claimed as the true explanation of his person was the only one of many possible descriptions which the early church failed to use! But at this point we discover how misleading it can be to assume that these various terms were already titles, for in spite of all attempts to prove the opposite, there is in fact no evidence that such a title was in existence in the time of Jesus. This particular phrase is well-known from Dan. 7.13, but there it is certainly not a title, only a description of the figure who appears in Daniel's vision, and who in contrast to the beasts is said to be 'like a Son of man'. Moreover, recent investigation has suggested that the phrase 'the Son of man' might have been used in first-century Aramaic as a way of referring to oneself – rather like the somewhat odd but nevertheless understandable use of 'one' today by those who really mean 'I'.[2]

We shall probably be totally misled, therefore, if we think of the phrase 'the Son of man' as a 'title' – either in the mind of Jesus himself, or for Mark. The problem of why Jesus himself used the term 'the Son of man', and what he meant by it, is an extremely complex one. It seems likely that there was something distinctive about his use of the phrase, or it would not have been remembered; it seems likely also that he adopted it in order to express his understanding of his own role. Fortunately we do not have to grapple with this particular problem here.[3] But what, we need to ask, did Mark understand by the phrase? Did he regard it simply as an odd quirk of Jesus' style? Or did he believe it had some real significance? When we examine the sayings in Mark's Gospel where the phrase is used, we find that twelve out of the fourteen are concerned with the theme of suffering and future vindication. We shall come back to this theme in a later chapter, but for the moment we may note that it is as the Son of man that Jesus must suffer – and be raised (8.31; 9.9, 12, 31; 10.33, 45; 14.21, 41). Three promises of future vindication all speak of the Son of man – and in every case the vindication follows persecution for either Jesus or his disciples (8.38; 13.26; 14.62). The remaining two sayings are about the authority exercised by the Son of man as God's representative on earth (2.10, 28). There is a remarkable similarity in theme between what is said about the Son of man in Mark, and the picture of the righteous remnant of Israel drawn in Dan. 7 – a picture of men and women suffering because of their obedience to God and because of the wickedness of their enemies, but finally vindicated (in the person of their representative, the 'one like a Son of man') by God himself.[4] In other words, what Jesus says about himself in Mark as Son of man fits the picture of God's obedient and suffering people in Daniel. It is misleading to suggest that Mark thinks of Jesus claiming the *title* of 'the Son of man'; it is truer to say that he shows Jesus accepting the role which belongs to that term.

But this means that in Mark's portrait, Jesus makes *no* direct claims for himself. In saying that the Son of man must suffer, Jesus accepts the way of suffering which obedience to God's will inevitably brings. In affirming that the Son of man will be vindicated, he expresses confidence in divine justice: God will vindicate his elect, who are faithful even to death. If he claims authority as the Son of man, this is because God has promised this authority to his faithful people. The use of the phrase 'the Son of man' in the mouth of Jesus as Mark presents it, is not a claim for messianic status, for privileges and honour: rather, it is an acknowledgment that God's will involves suffering, an avowal of obedience to that will, an affirmation of faith in God whatever happens, and a declaration of confidence that God will reward his trust in him. It is for others to acknowledge Jesus as God's Messiah; and it is only because he is content to accept the role of 'the Son of man' that he can be proclaimed as Messiah. So, when Peter declares him to be God's Anointed, and when the high priest asks if he is the Anointed, the Son of the Blessed, Jesus speaks instead of his mission as the Son of man – of one who is obedient to God's will and who is acknowledged by him.

Mark's picture, then, is more consistent than we at first supposed. The fact that Jesus refers to himself as 'the Son of man' does not destroy the secrecy that surrounds his identity. His acceptance of the role of suffering which is 'necessary' for the Son of man is part of the evidence that is spread out before his disciples, and which they fail to understand, because they cannot grasp that greatness belongs only to those who are humble and obedient. But it is also part of the evidence that Mark offers to his readers. Jesus is the one who obediently accepts suffering and trusts in God to vindicate him. Unless our eyes are blind and our hearts heardened, we shall recognize him as the one who is destined to receive 'dominion and glory and kingdom, that all peoples, nations and languages should serve him', for 'his dominion is an everlasting dominion, which shall not pass away, and his kingdom one that shall not be destroyed' (Dan. 7.14).

SIX

The Messiah and Israel

One of the intriguing things about the Gospels is the significant role played by John the Baptist. He appears at strategic points throughout the story, sometimes in somewhat surprising places. In John's Gospel, for example, he appears twice in the Prologue, interrupting the poetic structure of that section and causing commentators endless puzzlement. The two passages that refer to him, in John 1. 6–8, 15, have been described by one commentator as 'rude interruptions',[1] but the description is hardly fair; for if we analyse them, we find that here the Baptist plays his usual role of witness, testifying that Jesus is the one who was promised in the Old Testament and expected by Israel. In Mark, also, John appears at the very beginning of the story – indeed, *before* the beginning. The Gospel begins with him, and the account of Jesus' ministry begins with a reference to him, in v. 14. There is no doubt about the importance of his role as the forerunner of Jesus.

It is something of a surprise, after the opening fanfare of Mark's first three verses – 'The beginning of the gospel of Jesus Christ, as it is written in the prophet Isaiah . . .' to find ourselves reading about John the Baptist. It is even more remarkable, since as we have seen this is the only occasion in the Gospel where an Old Testament quotation is used in an editorial comment, rather than in the mouth of Jesus. The Gospel begins with the messenger, who prepares the way for the one who follows him; it is John who fulfils the words of the prophets. But if John fulfils the prophecies, preparing the way of the Lord, then he is the expected messenger; scripture and messenger combine to mark out the person who arrives next on the scene as the one who comes. John is an enigmatic figure, who belongs neither to the old order of the prophets (for he fulfils them) nor to the new order of the gospel (for he is its herald). His role is that of witness and forerunner.

John preaches in the wilderness, so fulfilling, in Mark's eyes, the prophecy in Isaiah 40 about the voice crying in the wilderness; his wild appearance and hairy garment, together with his wilderness diet, mark him out as a prophet. Malachi 4 promised that God would send the prophet Elijah before the final Day of the Lord, in order to call men to repentance: John preaches a baptism of repentance, and he speaks of the mighty one who will follow him, and who will baptize men with Holy Spirit. Malachi 3 describes the messenger who will come before the Lord – the Lord, who will come in power, and before whom none can stand. This is the scene set by Mark in the first eight verses of the Gospel. His mission is to prepare Israel for the coming of her Lord, and this he faithfully fulfils. The whole country of Judaea, and all the people of Jerusalem, too, flock to hear him preach. Mark means us to understand that God's messenger has been sent to Israel, and the whole of Israel has heard his message. The way for the coming one has been properly prepared.

No sooner does John appear in Mark's Gospel than he is done away with. The story of Jesus' ministry in Galilee begins with the arrest of John in v. 14; after the handing over of John, Jesus came, preaching the gospel. John is only the messenger who prepares the way; having preached repentance and announced the coming of someone greater, his task is done. Once Jesus appears on the scene, there is nothing further for John to do, and he is handed over to custody. But here already we see the other way in which John is to play the role of Jesus' forerunner, for the verb used here of John's arrest (*paradidōmi*, to hand over) is one that is used later in the story of the handing over and betrayal of Jesus.

In Mark 2.18f., we have an incident which refers to the disciples of John, and contrasts their behaviour to the behaviour of Jesus' own disciples. The story may perhaps reflect a tradition in which John and Jesus were presumed to be contemporaries; or even one in which Jesus was thought to be a disciple of John – hence the surprise at the very different behaviour of the two groups. Whatever the origin of the story, for Mark the contrast is between the Christian community on the one hand – a community marked by joy and celebration – and Judaism on the other (whether represented by the Pharisees or by the Baptist). John points forward to Jesus, but precisely because he points forward, he does not belong to the time of fulfilment.

In chapter 6, we have the only story in Mark's Gospel which is not directly about Jesus; it is, instead, about John the Baptist. Between the story of Jesus sending out his disciples to preach and heal, and the account of their return, Mark has placed the story of how the Baptist met his death. The insertion seems somewhat artificial; there is no logical link between the two stories, though Mark has made some attempt to make them tie up by describing the reaction of Herod to Jesus' fame: John, he declares, must have been raised from the dead. The story of John's death is told in unusual detail. Its purpose, of course, is to recount the fate of Jesus' forerunner. Just as John's arrest foreshadowed that of Jesus, so does his execution. Different though their two ends are, there is at least one similarity, in that both are put to death by rulers who recognize their goodness, but who weakly give way to pressure. No doubt Mark intends us also to see a contrast between the two endings of the story. John is beheaded, and his disciples come and bury him; and though Mark reports that rumours of his resurrection circulate, that is the end of John. It is an irony that Jesus should be rumoured to be a resurrected John; at this point John ceases to be Jesus' forerunner, for it needs a greater than John to be raised from the dead.

John appears again in chapter 9, though this time in disguise, as it were. In the transfiguration scene, Jesus speaks with two Old Testament characters – with Elijah and with Moses. Somewhat surprisingly, Elijah is mentioned first, though he was a later and less important figure for the Jews than Moses. Probably Mark mentions him first because the conversation on the way down the mountain is going to centre on him. Why it should be Moses and Elijah who meet with Jesus is the cause of endless speculation. The usual suggestion that they represent the Law and the prophets seems irrelevant. Perhaps they are appropriate figures because both of them experienced persecution and suffering; perhaps because both of them saw something of the glory of the Lord; perhaps because both of them were, according to Jewish legend, translated to heaven at the end of their lives – a tradition which, of course, contradicts the biblical account of Moses' death. The disciples, however, want to know, not why Elijah was on the mountain, but why the scribes say he must come 'first'. Presumably what is meant is 'before the Day of the Lord' – a reference to the Elijah tradition reflected in Mal. 4 to which I have already referred. Jesus replies that Elijah has already come, and that men have done to him what they wished, as it is written. It seems clear that Mark means us to understand that Elijah has come in the person of John the Baptist, and that what they have done to him is to execute him. Where this is written is, however, *not* clear, though perhaps the phrase 'what they wished' is meant to point us back to the hatred which Queen Jezebel had for Elijah (I Kings 19.2). The significance of what has happened to this new Elijah, however, lies in the fact that if men have done that to him, they will certainly do to the Son of man what is written of *him*. Elijah is indeed the forerunner who comes before the Lord, but though he has faithfully prepared the way, men have rejected his message. What, then, must we expect? Judgment and wrath? Perhaps – but these are not spoken of yet. First, the Son of man must follow in the path prepared by John. If the forerunner has been rejected, so too will the Son of man be rejected. If men have killed John, they are bound to kill Jesus also. The way to the eschatological glory glimpsed on the mountain is the same for them both – the way of suffering.

The link between the mission of John and that of Jesus is spelt out clearly by Mark in chapter 11. Jesus has arrived in Jerusalem; he has marched into the temple, and challenged the activities taking place there. The Jewish officials demand to know by what authority he is acting in this way: Who has given him authority to do these things? Jesus replies with another question: Was the baptism of John 'from heaven or from men?' – in other words, what was John's authority in baptizing repentant Israel? This counter-attack is not simply an attempt to change the subject. There is a link between the two questions, and if Jesus' questioners' get the right answer to his question, then they will have answered their own. Nor is it simply that the two cases of the Baptist and Jesus are analogous, since the mission of John is bound up with that of Jesus. He is the forerunner of Jesus, and the source of his authority to baptize must be the same as Jesus' own. We begin to see the significance of what is being said. If Jesus here points us back to the baptism of John, then what kind of claim does Mark understand him to be making for himself? If the mission of John is the key to understanding Jesus' activity, this can only mean that *he* is the one foretold by John – the mighty one who follows John but is far greater. For Mark's readers, the implication is clear. The true identity of Jesus, here as elsewhere in the Gospel, is plain to those who have eyes to see and ears to hear. Once again, John is the forerunner of the Lord, and witnesses to the one who follows him.

But perhaps we may take the matter further than this.

Back in chapter 1, Mark introduced John with a quotation from Mal. 3.1. The messenger in Malachi is sent to prepare the way of the Lord, who is going to arrive suddenly in his temple, where he will judge his people, and purify the sons of Levi until they offer proper offerings. Now, in chapter 11, Jesus arrives in the temple and acts in a way that seems very appropriate to that prophecy. Does Mark expect us to see a link between Mal. 3 and this scene, when he refers us back to the work of John the Baptist? It would be nice if we could make that link. But since there is no hint of the Malachi passage here, and since in chapter 1 Mark attributes the Malachi quotation to Isaiah, and makes no reference to the appearance of the Lord in the temple, we are clearly on shaky ground! The most that we can claim is that behind the story as Mark tells it there may perhaps have been a stage in the tradition when Mal. 3 played a part in linking the actions of Jesus in the temple with the questions about his authority and that of John the Baptist. Certainly we cannot maintain with any certainty that Mark himself was aware of the link.

There is one final reference to Elijah in Mark. Jesus' cry from the cross in 15.34 is misunderstood by the bystanders as a cry to Elijah for help. There is some evidence elsewhere in Jewish writings of a belief that Elijah would come to the aid of the godly in time of need. But Mark has already identified Elijah with John the Baptist. And unless he has forgotten that identification, there is surely irony in the suggestion that Elijah might come to the aid of Jesus. For Elijah himself has already been put to death, and there is no aid that he can offer.

Before we leave the theme of the role played by the Baptist in Mark's Gospel, it is worth noting one other Jewish tradition about Elijah. In some sources, he is expected to anoint the Messiah. One passage[2] says that Elijah is to restore three things that were hidden at the destruction of the temple – namely, the jar of manna, the flask of lustration and the flask of anointing oil. Justin Martyr, writing in the second century AD,[3] records the belief that Elijah is to come and anoint the Messiah, and then he is manifest to Israel. Perhaps it is a tradition of this kind that has influenced the Markan picture of John as the forerunner of Jesus. John may not actually anoint Jesus – except with water; Jesus is anointed with Holy Spirit. But certainly after the ministry of John, the Messiah is manifest – if not to Israel, then at least to the readers of Mark's Gospel.

But if John is sent to prepare Israel for the coming one, what goes wrong? Why does the nation fail to receive her Messiah? Notice first of all that Jesus accepts John's baptism, and so associates himself with the company of true Israelites who respond to his preaching. Jesus then appears in Galilee, and in spite of what is sometimes said about that region being Galilee of the Gentiles, his audience is a Jewish one: he teaches in their synagogues. Moreover, many of the miracles which Mark attributes to Jesus are more than acts of healing; for Jesus is dealing not simply with cases of illness, but with uncleanness – with various forms of defilement which cut men and women off from the Jewish community. The man with leprosy, the paralytic who needed forgiveness, the woman with a haemorrhage, the dead child, were all cut off, in one way or another, from the life of Israel. In healing them, Jesus brings back outcasts into the circle of those who belong to the people of God, restoring those who had been cut off from society. Jesus is shown bringing restoration to Israel, salvation to outsiders. In the debates between Jesus and the religious authorities, we have discussions about the behaviour which is proper to those who belong to this community: discussions about fasting (2.18), about sabbath observance (2.23–3.6), about the washing of hands (7.1). Perhaps it is significant that the debate about fasting in chapter 2 leads into the saying about new wine bursting old bottles and a new patch spoiling an old garment; Judaism cannot contain what is happening in Jesus. And in chapter 7, after a long debate between Jesus and the Pharisees about uncleanness, we have the story of an unclean Gentile woman who is allowed a crumb from the table, and who because of her faith is able to share the bread meant for Israel's children. Mark does not depict Jesus as going outside the Jewish nation – except on rare occasions which stand as exceptions. True, he does not move in the best circles; he is found in the company of sinners. But his mission is to Israel, and in particular to those who belong to Israel but have found themselves, for one reason or another, on the fringes of Jewish society. He seeks out the sinners, and is found in the company of riff-raff; instead of eating with Pharisees, he takes supper with tax-collectors. And in justification of this behaviour he talks about the sick needing a doctor (2.17), and about saving men's lives (3.4).

But though Jesus' mission is to Israel, his reception is hostile – at least by those who are *not* on the fringes of society. Pharisees and Herodians plot together to destroy him in 3.6; the scribes attribute his power to Satan in 3.22, and his own family and friends reject his claims; the citizens of his own town take offence at his words and activities. From the early chapters of Mark it is already plain that (to borrow John's phrase) 'his own did not receive him'.

What happens, however, when Jesus arrives in Jerusalem? He enters the city as a king, and is hailed as Son of David. His only action on arriving is to inspect the temple; then he retreats to Bethany for the night. The story of what takes place in the temple next day forms the middle section of one of Mark's 'sandwiches' – or, to put it in more technical language, he has intercalated it between the two parts of the story of the barren fig tree. It is clear that Mark intends us to read the two stories together. The story of the cursing of the fig tree is the last of the miracle stories in Mark – or rather, it is the antitype of a miracle story: instead of life, Jesus brings death, instead of restoration, destruction. The tree which fails to provide fruit when Jesus searches is for

Mark a symbol of what he finds when he looks for fruit in the temple. Just as the fig tree is barren, so is Israel's worship. Although Jesus' actions in the temple are frequently referred to as the cleansing of the temple, it seems better to recognize that for Mark, at least, what Jesus does is to condemn the worship of the temple rather than to reform it. He condemns those who have used the worship of God as an excuse for profiteering, and so prevented others from offering true worship. The link with the story of the fig tree shows clearly that Mark sees what happens as a prophetic sign of coming judgment and destruction; the barren tree is cursed and withers; Israel's barren worship heralds the destruction of the temple. The withered tree is an appropriate symbol for this destruction, since in Jewish literature the withering of fig trees and the failure to produce fruit are often used to symbolize the judgment of Yahweh on Israel and his condemnation of her corrupt worship.[4] Moreover, the opposite idea is true: the fruitful tree is a symbol of blessing, and the messianic age will be marked by tremendous productivity. When Jesus the Messiah comes to Jerusalem and looks for fruit on the fig tree, ought he not to find some? True, it is not the season for figs – but what matter? The messianic age, the time of harvest is here; this is why the fig tree is condemned. It is a fitting symbol for Israel, who fails to respond when her Messiah comes to her.

Whether it was Mark who was responsible for interpreting Jesus' actions in the temple as a sign of destruction rather than of restoration I do not know. It is possible that the tradition had this significance already – possible, indeed, that the original incident had this character. What *is* clear – or ought to be be! – is that Mark has underlined this meaning for us in his presentation of the material. The intercalation of the story between the two parts of the fig tree story betrays Mark's hand: Jesus' teaching to the disciples when they find the tree withered is meant to be seen by the reader as a comment on the central story. The Lord has come to his temple, and found only corruption and barren worship; the Messiah has come to Israel, and the people have failed to respond. Their failure makes judgment and destruction inevitable.

This double-decker story is followed by the one we have already examined, the incident in the temple where the leaders of Israel question Jesus about his authority to act in this way. And perhaps now we have discovered a good reason why Mark does *not* make use of the tradition from Mal. 3 about the Lord coming suddenly to his temple; for though that passage speaks about this coming in terms of a refining fire, the end of the story there is that the temple is restored, and the offering of Judah and Jerusalem is once again found pleasing to the Lord. For Mark, there is no such happy outcome for the Jerusalem temple.

Chapter 12 brings us another parable. Unlike the earlier parables in chapter 4, this one is directed to the opponents of Jesus, who have just challenged his authority; moreover, they understand clearly its meaning. Or at least – they understand that it is directed at them (v. 12). They realize that the wicked tenants in the parable represent the leaders of the nation and that the message of the parable is that they must expect divine judgment and punishment. And their punishment is to be final. 'What will the owner of the vineyard do? He will come and destroy the tenants, and give the vineyard to others.' But at another level, they certainly do not understand. The final messenger sent to the tenants is the owner's beloved son – to readers of the Gospel, a clear reference to Jesus himself, who has already twice been addressed from heaven as God's beloved Son. Whether Mark thinks of Jesus' opponents recognizing this as a veiled messianic claim is not clear; certainly he does not say that they did – only that they realized he was attacking *them*. Once again we have the secret of Jesus' identity. To us, the clue is plain: Jesus is the beloved son, and it is because the leaders of Israel reject his claims that they bring punishment on their own heads; Israel's rejection of her Messiah leads in turn to her own rejection. But that is not quite the end of the story. The vineyard will be given to 'others'. The fact that Israel's leaders prove themselves unworthy cannot frustrate the purpose of God. The proof-text which rounds off the story hints at the new building which is going to be erected, with the rejected stone as its chief foundation. The mixture of metaphors hints at the way in which the idea of Israel as the Lord's vineyard or vine is parallel to the theme of the temple as the place of his worship. The temple mount may be removed,[5] and the temple itself be destroyed, but a new worshipping community will emerge, built on the risen Lord.

Mark ends this account of Jesus' teaching in Jerusalem with his commendation of the widow woman who throws everything she has into the temple treasury. Jesus has just condemned those scribes whose religion is a sham (vv. 38–40); this woman, by contrast, demonstrates that she loves God with her whole heart and her neighbour as herself, and her gift is therefore worth far more than the gifts and sacrifices of the other worshippers. By her action, she has shown her understanding of the greatest of the commandments (cf. vv. 28–34).

Following after all this, the prophecy of Jerusalem's destruction in chapter 13 is no surprise. It is true that no explanation is given in this chapter as to why the temple is to be razed to the ground – but we hardly need one. It is clear that the coming devastation will be the punishment for Israel's disobedience, and in particular for her failure to respond to her Messiah. But before that takes place, Jesus' own followers must expect to suffer persecution; it is not only the Messiah himself who will be rejected, but the messianic community. Finally, when the punishment is complete, the Son of man will vindicate the elect and gather them into God's kingdom.

The story of Jesus in Jerusalem is a story of rejection and the story has two strands. On the one hand, Israel rejects her Messiah. True, the people who accompany Jesus into Jerusalem hail him as the one who comes in the name of the Lord, but Mark suggests that they belong to Jesus' own company – they are those who go before and those who follow, and they do not belong to Jerusalem. True, the crowds in Jerusalem listen to Jesus teaching in the temple, and ask him questions – but most of them are hostile questions. The story of the withered fig tree and the parable of the vineyard tenants show, moreover, that Mark understands Israel already to have rejected her Messiah. The second strand in the theme of rejection is the rejection of Israel herself. Because she rejects Jesus, she will in turn be rejected. This is the first time that we have met the theme of punishment in Mark. We had a hint of it in 3.29, in the saying about sinning against the Holy Spirit; we had the sayings about Gehenna in 9.42ff. But not even John the Baptist, in Mark, speaks about future punishment. The impact is all the greater when the tree is blighted, the temple put in disarray, and the future fate of the people spelt out in chapter 13.

The theme of Israel's rejection of her Messiah comes to a climax in the trial scene. Jesus was brought before the high priest of Israel, and the whole Sanhedrin sought testimony against him, in order to put him to death, but they could find none, for he was innocent. They therefore resorted to false witnesses. Mark tells us that their testimony did not agree – a comment which is perhaps intended to underline the fact that their testimony was false. Their accusations concern the destruction and rebuilding of the temple: Jesus, they say, has threatened to destoy the temple, and claimed that he can build another in three days. There is, of course, no such saying in Mark's Gospel. We have had the violent actions of Jesus in the temple, which seem to symbolize its destruction, and we have had the prophecy of Jesus, spoken in private, to four disciples, that the temple will be destroyed; and there has been a hint of a rebuilding, in chapter 12, after the parable of the vineyard. The accusation is a distortion of Jesus' words, since the witnesses are false. It is not Jesus who will destroy the temple, it is the Jews themselves, since in rejecting Jesus and attempting to destroy *him*, they are bringing inevitable punishment on themselves. The accusation they bring against him should be brought against their own nation. The fascinating thing about these false charges is that they once again tie up the fate of Israel (symbolized by the temple) and the fate of the Messiah. Destroy one, and you destroy the other. Israel has rejected her salvation. Only in this sense is Jesus the cause of her destruction. In trying to destroy her Messiah, Israel destroys herself.

Since the court has failed to make these accusations against Jesus stick, the high priest resorts to other means. He challenges Jesus directly, inviting him to condemn himself out of his own mouth; and when Jesus replies, he accuses him of blasphemy. The high priest tears his garments – and so do the commentators! It was not legal, they protest, to challenge a prisoner in this way; and the words attributed to Jesus do not constitute blasphemy. Well, perhaps that is the point. Perhaps Mark knew it as well as the commentators. Of course the charge is false – like the evidence of the witnesses; of course the proceedings are illegal. The whole scene is a farce. Jesus is on trial before the high priest, but in fact it is Israel who is on trial; it is not Jesus who breaks the Law but his opponents, who claim to uphold it. It is not Jesus who condemns himself out of his own mouth, but the high priest who condemns himself by his actions. The death warrant that Caiaphas signs may bear the name of Jesus – but it brings doom to Israel, and it is Israel that is judged and condemned. And at the very moment when Jesus' own fate seems sealed, he announces his vindication: the Son of man will be seen at God's right hand, and coming in clouds to judge his people.

So we come to the account of the crucifixion, and at the climax of the story, when Jesus dies, Mark tells us that the curtain of the temple was torn in two, from top to bottom. What significance does Mark see in this rending of the curtain? Does he see it as a symbol of the temple's destruction? Is it the end of the sacrificial system? Or the end of the nation? Or is it perhaps a symbol of something more positive? If the curtain separating the Holy of Holies from the rest of the temple is torn, does this imply that a new way into God's presence has been created? All these ideas are used in different places in the New Testament. In view of all that has been said about the temple in Mark's Gospel, it seems likely that the symbol is meant to point us once again to the destruction of the temple. But that is not totally negative. Always there are signs of hope. Temple worship is corrupt – but a poor widow offers all she has; the leaders of the nation reject Jesus – but the vineyard will be given to others. Jerusalem will be destroyed – but the Son of man will gather his elect. The curtain is torn in two as Jesus dies, but his executioner declares: 'This man was indeed Son of God.' From now on, it is no longer a question of Gentile dogs eating the crumbs that fall from the table. Israel has rejected her Messiah, but his death marks a new beginning; it is 'for many'. From now on, the gospel must be preached to all the nations (13.10). The vineyard is given to others.

SEVEN

The Death of Jesus

Mark's Gospel has been described as a passion narrative with a long introduction. Exaggeration though this may be, it is nevertheless a fair reminder of the way in which the death of Jesus dominates the story. Indeed, one wonders which chapters one should allocate to the passion narrative, and which to the introduction. Strictly speaking, the passion narrative begins at 14.1. Yet there is a sense in which it begins at 11.1, when Jesus arrives in Jerusalem. Indeed, the death of Jesus is the dominant theme as early as 8.31, and even before this there are hints of what lies in store.

Why should so much of Mark's Gospel be given over to this theme? Is it simply a reflection of the way in which the gospel was preached? After all, Paul has a great deal more to say about the death and resurrection of Jesus than about his ministry. Even before the emphasis shifted to seeing Mark as a theologian, commentators were inclined to believe that the reason for his choice of material here was a theological one – that is, that he wished to stress this theme for some particular reason. The traditional explanations for this emphasis have taken two forms. On the one hand, it is possible that Mark wrote as he did in order to deal with a doctrinal problem – namely, the idea of a crucified Messiah. Was Mark perhaps writing for those who found it difficult to see how Jesus could be the Messiah if he was crucified, or crucified if he was the Messiah? Paul describes the message of a crucified Messiah as a stumbling block for Jews, and so it must have been. On the other hand, the problem might have been a practical one. Was the Markan community suffering persecution? If so, then the emphasis throughout the later chapters of Mark on the necessity for the disciple to follow in the steps of his crucified Lord would be a useful encouragement. Hence the familiar link-up with the idea that Mark was writing for the church of Rome – though the link may well be a jump, for there were plenty of other Christian communities besides that in Rome which had to endure persecution. Recently, however, very different suggestions have been made about the problem that led Mark to lay so much emphasis on this theme. Again, we have a choice between a doctrinal and a practical problem – though as usual these two may well be linked, rather than being exclusive. On the doctrinal level, it is suggested that Mark's community, far from worrying about how the Messiah could be crucified, had conveniently chosen to ignore the message of the cross. Carried away by enthusiasm in proclaiming the power of their Lord, they had forgotten his humility and weakness; they worshipped a risen and ascended Lord, but not a crucified one. Now the precise form in which this thesis has been argued seems to me very dubious indeed.[1] We have seen already that there is no evidence to suggest that Mark thought of Peter's acknowledgment of Jesus as Messiah as wrong; nor is there any sign of his having 'played down' the idea of a miracle worker. But certainly he wishes to persuade his readers that there is more to be said about Jesus than that he is Messiah, or a worker of mighty miracles! Amazement at the power of Jesus is not enough. The crowds were amazed, but they were far from understanding the gospel. Or perhaps the problem is primarily a practical one – concern about the behaviour of Christians who had forgotten that their faith was based on the death of Jesus. Were those in Mark's community, far from suffering persecution, in fact having a rather easy life, and behaving in a manner very little different from that of their pagan neighbours? Does this explain the emphasis on the call to take up the cross and follow Jesus?

This is a question to which we must return, when we have looked at the way in which Mark handles the theme. If he is dealing with the problem of how the Messiah could be crucified, then we would expect him to answer the problem 'Why?' It is not enough simply to proclaim that Jesus *is* the Messiah, in spite of the crucifixion. Our very earliest records suggest that from the beginning Christian preachers attempted to demonstrate that it was *necessary* for the Messiah to suffer in this way – contrary to all expectations. Certainly the first major emphasis that we notice in looking at the way in which Mark handles the death of Christ is the insistence on its *inevitability*.

For Mark, this means first of all, of course, that the death of Christ is part of the divine purpose. It is inconceivable that God's Messiah should have suffered *unless* God had so willed. However strange or mysterious it may be, the death of Jesus must be part of the divine will. Mark emphasizes this in every passion prediction: the Son of man *must* suffer (8.31); it is written of the Son of man (9.12); the Son of man *will be* delivered up (9.31; 10.33). The outcome of Jesus' journey to Jerusalem is certain – because God has so decreed; and if it is part of God's plan, then we may expect to find it foreshadowed in scripture. But secondly, Jesus dies because he accepts the divine plan and is obedient to it. He does not *have* to go to Jerusalem – he himself deliberately set out on the road. In Caesarea Philippi he is about as far to the north as his ministry ever takes him. But from that point onwards he is heading for Jerusalem. Jesus clearly foresees his sufferings, according to Mark, but he accepts them as his destiny; they are the cup which he must drink and the baptism with which he must be baptized. But there is a third strand in this theme of inevitability. For the death of Jesus is due to the wickedness of men – to their refusal to accept Jesus as their Messiah, and their rejection of his authority. It is due also to the treachery of Judas, whose act of betrayal gives the Jewish leaders the opportunity they require. It may perhaps seem contradictory to maintain at one and the same time that the death of Jesus is due to the working out of God's purposes and also to the disobedience of men, which frustrates those purposes; that the goodness of God and the wickedness of men work towards the same end. Yet we find Mark combining them: 'The Son of man goes as it is written of him; but woe to that man through whom he is betrayed' (14.21). But truth is often paradoxical, and certainly we can understand how Mark can maintain two interpretations which might at first seem contradictory. We find the same tension elsewhere in Mark: if men refuse to hear Jesus and to respond to his word, that is because God has hardened their hearts. The truth must have been hidden from them – nothing else can explain the 'failure' of Jesus' mission. The prophet Isaiah had a similar experience, referred to in Mark 4.12. But that does not excuse those who harden their hearts and stop their ears and eyes to the truth; their guilt remains.

Mark's judgment is made with the benefit of hindsight. Fortunately we do not have to determine how the participants in the drama might have seen things. At the very least, one must say that he has exaggerated all three strands in this theme. Certainly at the time it had been anything but clear that the cross was part of God's plan; it is difficult to know whether the hearts of the Jewish leaders were *quite* as obtuse as Mark suggests, or to assess what part they played in the events. As for Jesus himself, the problem of the extent to which he foresaw his own suffering and death is a familiar one. But to say this is not to pass judgment on whether or not Mark has got things right. It often happens that events become meaningful only as we look back on them. Happenings which seem at the time mere coincidence, purposeless, even tragic, sometimes take on a very different appearance at a later stage in one's life. Those involved in the making of history often do not realize the importance of their actions. How many of the Battle of Britain pilots could have known just how important a role they were playing in the Second

World War? Just as some things which dominate our lives sometimes look trivial when we look back on them, so it is difficult to realize the full importance of other events, which later are seen to have been crucial. Certainly the disciples saw the death of Jesus in a totally new light after the resurrection. And since we, like Mark, stand on this side of the resurrection, we cannot put ourselves back into the historical situation; we can only look at events in the light of later knowledge. In terms of historical verisimilitude, many of Mark's scenes creak. We find it difficult to believe that Jesus predicted his death in such detail; impossible to believe that the disciples were incapable of understanding the plain meaning of these words. But Mark looks back on the death of Jesus and sees its significance for Christian believers. He is sure that God's purpose was achieved through the cross – and that it must therefore have been part of the divine plan; he is sure that Jesus was obedient to God's will – and that he must have understood where that would take him; as for those who put God's Messiah to death, they are guilty of sinning against the Holy Spirit, and for their guilt there can be no excuse.

In these three ways, then, Mark deals with the question 'Why did Jesus die?' But so far, he has answered it only in the sense of 'How did it come about that?' How did it come about that God's Messiah was put to death? When an agonized mother asks 'Why did my child die?' it is no answer to her anguish to reply, 'Because he ran out into the road after a ball'; or, 'Because a careless driver did not keep a proper lookout.' It is worse than useless to suggest that the child's death can be attributed to the will of God. The mother is looking for meaning in an apparently meaningless event; she is looking for something which will transform tragedy by finding in it a source of comfort. To blame the child, or the driver, or even God, cannot provide that. Surprisingly, the evangelists seem to give us very little in the way of an answer to this deeper question. Perhaps one reason is that for them, the answer is found in the resurrection. This was what transformed tragedy into triumph and brought sense out of nonsense. It may be that for some time this was the only answer given by Christian preachers to the question 'Why?' in this deeper sense. By and large it was later theologians who explored the meaning of Christ's death, and who emphasized its power as atonement for sin. At first sight, Mark has almost nothing to say about the death of Christ in this light. The famous exception is, of course, the saying in Mark 10.45: 'The Son of man did not come to be served but to serve, and to give his life as a ransom for many.' But how did Mark understand these words – the only saying about the meaning of the cross that he attributes to Jesus?

Now this question is not as straightforward as it seems. Most commentators suggest that the saying reflects the language of Isa. 53, and that Mark is thinking of Jesus' mission in terms of the so-called 'Servant' whose sufferings bring forgiveness to others. In fact, however, the language of Mark 10.45 shows hardly any resemblance to that of Isa. 53, and only the word 'many' is common to both.[2] More important still, the ideas in the two passages are different. We tend to assume that Mark 10.45 is a saying about the forgiveness of sins, since the idea of Christ dying for others is inevitably linked in our minds with the experience of forgiveness, but neither sin nor forgiveness is mentioned here. The Son of man gives his life as a *ransom*. The background of the word used here, *lutron*, is certainly to be found in the Old Testament, in the belief that God ransomed his people from slavery in Egypt at the Exodus. Now, in some mysterious way, the death of Jesus is to achieve the same for the new people of God. His death is to be *for many*. Again, we tend to see this in terms of the multitude of redeemed sinners. But the word 'many' may have a more specialized meaning than that. Evidence from the Qumran documents suggests that 'many' was an appropriate term to use of the righteous community, the members of God's covenant people. For us, the term 'many' means 'a lot of individuals'; perhaps for Mark it is more likely to have conveyed the sense of 'all those who belong to the one community'.

But there is a second reason why Mark apparently offers little help in thinking about why Jesus died And that is that we may be looking for the wrong thing. Perhaps we do not recognize the answers Mark gives for what they are. There is a well-known saying about Luke's Gospel to the effect that Luke has no theology of the cross.[3] What is meant, of course, is that Luke did not interpret the death of Christ in ways familiar to twentieth-century Christians. Now there are two things that have to be said in reply to this judgment. The first is, that what is said about Luke, in so far as it *is* true about Luke, is *almost* as true of the other evangelists as well; none of them has a great deal to say about the death of Jesus as an atonement for sins. The second is that there is in fact a great deal in Luke's Gospel about the significance of Jesus' death, but that it is spelt out in ways that would have made sense to first-century Christians soaked in the traditions of the Old Testament, and so is often lost on the modern reader. It may be, then, that Mark's failure to offer us an explanation of the death of Jesus, or to draw out its significance, is only apparent. It is worth investigating other themes which are found in the passion narrative in order to find out.

The first thing we need to notice is the context in which the various passion predictions are set. All of them are linked with the theme of leadership, of power and glory. The very first, of course, appears side-by-side with Peter's acknowledgment of Jesus as the Messiah. No sooner has Peter said, 'You are the Christ', than Jesus apparently changes the subject, and begins to teach the disciples about the suffering of the Son of man (8.31). The prediction in 9.12 is linked closely with the transfiguration scene. Later in the same chapter, 9.31 immediately precedes the dispute among the disciples about greatness; similarly, 10.33 is followed by the request of James and John to sit at Jesus' right and left hands in glory – and Jesus' answer leads into the saying in 10.45. There is a built-in paradox about the death of Jesus in Mark's presentation: it is seen as the *sine qua non* of his glory. Moreover, it is worth noting that strictly speaking it is inaccurate to describe these sayings as 'passion predictions'; perhaps the fact that we use this term so often means that we get things out of focus. The predictions are not only about the death of Jesus, but about his resurrection also; not only about his suffering, but about his vindication. The resurrection is mentioned in all four of these passages. Perhaps it is because there is so much material about the death of Jesus in chapters 14–15 that we tend to describe this whole section as the passion narrative, and to speak of the passion predictions. Or perhaps it is because later theologians have singled out the death of Jesus in speaking about the work of Christ and man's redemption – but it is worth asking whether we are distorting Mark's picture when we do so.

Let us look at the story as Mark unfolds it, beginning from the final prediction of death and resurrection in 10.33. Jesus is on the road for Jerusalem – and we know what *that* means. He spells out, more fully than ever before, what awaits him there; and immediately, James and John ask for a share in his glory. Like the rest of the disciples, the sons of Zebedee are pictured by Mark as uncomprehending when it comes to the theme of suffering, but the question attributed to them shows clearly that in Mark's mind there is an essential link between the death of Jesus and his glory. Only those who drink his cup and share his baptism can share his glory – because that is the way that he himself must go: it is through suffering that he gains the throne. So the incident leads into instruction from Jesus to his disciples about what it means to exercise authority in the Christian community. It can only be exercised through service, for that is how the Son of man himself 'has become great'.

According to this story, the disciples are thinking of Jesus as one who is destined to be a ruler among men. So, too, does Bartimaeus in the next incident. As Jesus leaves Jericho, Bartimaeus addresses him as 'Son of David'. Apart from Peter, Bartimaeus is the first person in Mark's Gospel to recognize Jesus as the Messiah. Now Bartimaeus is blind, and of course he may have got it wrong – but Jesus does not rebuke him; it is the crowd that tries to silence him. Jesus responds to the man's faith, and he follows the one whom he has greeted as king to Jerusalem.

The first thing that happens when Jesus arrives at Jerusalem is that he enters the city as a king. It is, of course, a very strange king who arrives on a donkey instead of a horse. The crowds hail Jesus as one who comes in the name of the Lord, and speaks of the coming kingdom of David. The words 'Hosanna, Blessed be he who comes in the name of the Lord' were a customary greeting to pilgrims arriving for the Passover, and it was natural that the Passover crowd should look forward to the coming Davidic kingdom. If their words had no deeper conscious significance than this, then the crowd need not have been as fickle as is sometimes suggested. But for Mark, the words are an acknowledgment of Jesus as king. Mark does not help us by spelling out his biblical references in the way that Matthew does, but it is difficult to believe that he was unaware of what is said about the king of Zion in Zech. 9.9, or that when he describes the crowds as spreading garments in the road before Jesus, he thought of them as doing anything but consciously welcoming him as their king. Jesus enters Jerusalem, as he left Jericho, to the plaudits of the crowd and hailed as Son of David.

In these three stories, then, we see Jesus acknowledged as king of some kind. True, none of those involved have any kind of idea as to what sort of a king he is, or how he will be proclaimed king. But they are not wrong in greeting him as such. In coming to Jerusalem, Jesus comes as king. Once there, we have a series of incidents that are concerned in some way or another with the authority of Jesus. He challenges the religious authorities of Israel to accept him, and they refuse. Their refusal makes his death inevitable. Of particular interest for our theme is the parable of the vineyard tenants in chapter 12, and the fate of the owner's only son. The story ought to end in v. 9, with the punishment of the tenants, but instead it leads into a quotation from Ps. 118: 'The stone which the builders rejected has become the head of the corner; this was the Lord's doing, and it is marvellous in our eyes.' The quotation does not really fit here at all; the rejected messengers of the parable are in no way 'built up'. But because the parable is really an allegory, it seems to need a reference to God's vindication of Jesus. Clearly it seemed unsatisfactory to leave the story with the only son having been killed and cast out of the vineyard; so it has been rounded off with a proof-text about the resurrection – and we have a glorious mixed metaphor as a result, since the son of the vineyard owner has become the foundation stone of a new temple. Now we cannot argue that Mark is responsible for this juxtaposition, for in the Gospel of Thomas, also, the parable is followed by the same proof text,[4] and it seems unlikely that Thomas was influenced by Mark. Clearly someone before Mark felt that it was unsatisfactory to leave a clear reference to the death of Jesus without rounding the story off. The rejected stone is made head of the corner: it is only through suffering that Jesus can be exalted.

The passion narrative proper begins in chapter 14 with the story of the anointing of Jesus by a woman at supper. This narrative provides an interesting example of the way in which a story could be adapted and given different interpretations by different evangelists. Luke, for example, places the story in a totally different context, and interprets the woman's action as the loving response of a forgiven sinner. For Mark, however, the primary significance of the story is the way in which the woman's action points forward to

Jesus' imminent death. Indeed, since in 16.1 the attempt to anoint his corpse is frustrated by his resurrection, this premature action symbolizes the fact that in his case the normal ceremony will not take place: Jesus is anointed for burial before death because he will not be anointed after death – and he will not be anointed then because God will raise him from the dead. The woman's action is thus a summary of the gospel, and this is why it will be recalled wherever the gospel is preached. Typically, Mark sandwiches the story between the two sections describing the authorities' plot to arrest Jesus – a reminder that the events that are now taking place are the result of more than merely human plans.

But Mark may well have seen another significance in this story. Jesus has entered Jerusalem as king; he is about to be challenged as to whether he is the Messiah by the high priest, and crucified as king of the Jews. It seems likely that Mark interpreted this anointing for burial as the symbol of Jesus' messianic anointing also. If so, we see how closely the themes of Jesus' death and his kingship are woven together. It is in being anointed for burial that Jesus is anointed as Messiah. The fact that the ritual was performed by a woman rather than by a priest is just one more anomaly in a story that is already anomalous from beginning to end.

It is clear from the description Mark gives in 14.12–17 of the preparation made by the disciples for the Last Supper that he interprets it as a celebration of the Passover. The problems of understanding the tradition here, of tracing its history and discovering its meaning, are so complex that they require a book on their own. We can only note the way in which the death of Jesus is once again described as being 'for many', and linked on the one hand to the theme of the covenant, on the other to the coming of God's kingdom.

The account of Jesus in Gethsemane shows him overcome with horror and dismay. It is an amazing picture. It has sometimes been suggested that this story was used to encourage Christians facing persecution. But it hardly seems suited for that – not, at least, in the way that Mark tells it. Jesus is overcome with horror, and shrinks from the prospect of death. This is not the sort of story you retell to encourage men to face up to death. It stands in remarkable contrast to stories about the calm with which Socrates met death, or about the courage of the Maccabean martyrs, or about the joy of early Christians dying because of their loyalty to their master. But of course, the story reflects the horror with which any Jew would have contemplated an early, violent death – for such a death was a sign of the displeasure, indeed the wrath, of God.

Mark tells us that Jesus is greatly distressed. It is the first time that he has hinted at the severity of the struggle. About the temptation, he told us simply that Jesus was tested by Satan. Now he is tested again, for this is the hour of temptation, the eschatological hour when the conflict with evil takes place: it is here, rather than on the cross, that the battle is fought. The words of Jesus' prayer echo the words of the prayer he taught to his disciples (though not in Mark): 'Father . . . what you will.' The reference to the cup echoes the words spoken to James and John, when he asked them if they were able to drink his cup. Now Jesus himself shrinks from the cup. We have here a strange contradiction with that earlier theme, which insisted on the inevitability of Jesus' sufferings. If death is inevitable, why does Jesus now shrink from it? How can the cup pass from him, if this has been part of his mission from the very beginning? Mark makes no attempt to resolve this conflict; the two ideas are held together in tension. In John the tension is solved by emphasizing one idea at the expense of the other. The fourth evangelist gives us no scene of agony in Gethsemane. Instead, we have the prayer of Jesus in 12.27: 'Shall I say, Father, save me from this hour? No, for this purpose I came to this hour.' It looks very much as though what has happened is that the idea stressed by Mark of the inevitability of Jesus' sufferings has gradually gained ground at the expense of the earlier picture of Jesus as uncertain about what lay in store for him. And surely this *is* the earlier picture. For it is the story of Gethsemane that rings true. It depicts the agony of someone who has hoped for success, and now realizes that his mission is doomed, rather than the dismay of someone who has always believed death to be inevitable and now begins to weaken. If we find problems with the Markan picture of Jesus as one who assumed death to be the inevitable outcome of his ministry, we may perhaps feel that the despair we glimpse in this scene is closer to the experience of Jesus himself, as he realized that if he was to remain faithful to his calling, death was now inevitable.

There is, of course, no reason to doubt that Jesus had reckoned with the *possibility* of failure and death long before this; he must have known well enough that to go to Jerusalem probably meant putting his head into a noose. He must have realized that faithfulness to the commands of God was likely to lead to a collision with the authorities, and so to failure and death. Many prophets and martyrs before him had met that fate. But had he throughout his ministry been without hope that Israel would respond to his call? Had he not hoped and prayed to the end that Israel might repent and turn to God, as men had repented at the preaching of Jonah? He had preached the kingdom of God – the rule of God – and had called on men to accept that kingdom; he must have hoped that they would respond to his call. If so, then perhaps to the end, there were two possible outcomes to Jesus' mission. One would mean success: men would have responded – Israel would have returned to God. The other would mean failure: if Israel refused to accept the rule of God, their obstinacy and sin would inevitably lead to suffering and death for him, and their own rejection by God. And now there is no hope. Unless God intervenes in some way, the outcome is inevitable. Jesus' mission has failed, and death for him – and for his nation – is inevitable. If this was the agony of Jesus, then it was agony indeed. It was the agony of one who – like Isaiah – is faced with the realization of failure; he has preached to people who have been deaf and blind, and who have failed to respond. He has preached the kingdom of God, and spoken of God acting in salvation and judgment; but where are that salvation and judgment now, and where are the signs of God's coming kingdom?

But of course, in asking questions about Jesus' own experience we must be content to ask questions and leave the matter there. We are concerned with Mark's understanding of these events. And from this angle, it is interesting to notice that there does seem to be a different tradition being used here that does not accord with his emphasis elsewhere. Yet in a sense it supports Mark's general theme. For the scene in Gethsemane stresses above all the obedience of Jesus to God's will. Though he may pray for the cup to pass, there is no suggestion that he will refuse to drink it; the disciples may fail, and fall asleep at the crucial hour, but Jesus is obedient, however bitter the cup may be. Tradition which seems at first sight to be in tension with Mark's main emphasis, and to have a very different origin, nevertheless serves his purpose.

If the scene in Gethsemane underlines the obedience of Jesus, the arrest demonstrates the responsibility of those who bring about his death at a human level – here the treachery of Judas, who betrays his master with a kiss, is underlined – and the belief that everything takes place in accordance with scripture. The flight of the disciples and the denial of Peter fulfil not only the words of scripture, but the prophecy of Jesus himself; the course of the drama is inevitable.

The final scene before the crucifixion itself is the trial before the high priest. It reaches a climax when the high priest challenges Jesus with the question, 'Are you the Christ, the Son of the Blessed?', and Jesus replies 'I am'. Historically, the account of the trial raises all kinds of problems. But theologically, it hangs together. For who else beside the high priest can proclaim God's chosen one as the Messiah? No matter that the high priest himself does not believe the proclamation. It is because Jesus acknowledges that he is Messiah that he is condemned to death. And it is *as* Messiah that he is put to death. The theme of kingship here comes to the fore. 'Are you the king of the Jews?', asks Pilate, when Jesus is brought before him. And then, to the crowd, 'What shall I do with the man whom you call the king of the Jews?' The soldiers clothe Jesus in purple, give him a crown of thorns and hail him as king of the Jews. Finally, the inscription of the charge on the cross reads, 'The king of the Jews'. It is as king that Jesus dies – through death that he is acknowledged as Messiah – even though those who hail him do so in mockery. Priests and scribes join forces to taunt him: 'Let the Christ, the king of Israel, come down now from the cross, that we may see and believe.' But here is the final irony; for were Jesus to come down from the cross, he would not be the Christ, the king of Israel; it is only through his death that men see and believe. And the first to believe is the Roman centurion, who watches him die and acknowledges him – not, indeed, as king of the Jews, but by a greater title: 'This man was indeed Son of God.'

As for Jesus himself, the only sentence he utters from the cross is that terrible cry: 'My God, my God, why have you forsaken me?' Christians have frequently recoiled from these words. Commentators have pointed out that they are the opening words of a psalm which ends in more hopeful vein; are we not intended, they ask, to remember the whole psalm? The answer is 'No', for there is no hint in Mark that he means us to do so; and if we follow this suggestion, we shall miss the point. Mark presents us with a picture of Jesus as utterly desolate – draining the cup of suffering to the dregs; it is of a piece with the picture of Jesus in Gethsemane, for here we see Jesus experiencing the bitterest blow known to the religious man – the sense of having been let down by God. Once again, the picture hardly fits with the usual Markan emphasis on Jesus going steadfastly towards an inevitable death, and it may well be that here too the evangelist is using earlier tradition which does not quite accord with his picture. Why, then, has he included it? Is it simply that he has taken over an early version of the crucifixion story? We must, of course, always remember the danger of reading too much into the material, and assuming that it represents some important element in Mark's theology when in fact he may simply have inherited it. Or did he perhaps include it because of the reference to Elijah? Or is it perhaps that Mark has no wish to sentimentalize the cross, or to ignore the reality of Jesus' sufferings?

And perhaps there *was* a danger that those who read his story might do just that. For the answer which has emerged to the question 'Why did Jesus die?' as we have skimmed through these final pages of his Gospel is that he died *in order that* he might be proclaimed as Messiah. It was not that Jesus died *in spite of* the fact that he was Messiah; rather, he died in order to be enthroned as Messiah. Those who wish to be great must be least; those who wish to rule must serve; those who wish to save their life must abandon it – and if that is true for Jesus' followers, it is true for him also. Jesus is hailed as king when he enters Jerusalem in lowliness, anointed as Messiah when he is anointed for burial, proclaimed as Israel's king by the high priest when he is condemned to death, believed in as Son of God when he dies. The cross has become the Messiah's throne – and that is a theme that could easily lead (and later *did* lead) to interpretations of the death of Jesus which played down the theme of suffering. But Mark, living in a world where the cross was a very real symbol of pain and humiliation, and where crucifixion was the most excruciating and humiliating form of capital punishment known to man, could scarcely forget the agony of Jesus: once again, the cry of dereliction which he attributes to Jesus rings true.

If we now go back to the question raised at the beginning

and ask *why* Mark emphasized the death of Jesus in this way, it seems that we are no nearer a solution. Clearly a good case can be made for saying that Mark wished to explain the scandal of the cross and that he felt his story would offer support to those facing persecution. But one can see, also, how his Gospel would be appropriate in a situation where Christians were *forgetting* the scandal of the cross and its implications – and if that seems an unlikely situation in the first century AD, we have only to remember what seems to have been going on in Corinth, even before Mark wrote his Gospel. Either suggestion fits – but that seems to tell us more about the relevance of the Gospel in any age than about the original purpose Mark had in writing it.

EIGHT

'If Anyone would be My Disciple ...'

Mark's Gospel is the good news about Jesus Christ. But it is also a story about discipleship. In contrast to the majority of Israel, who reject their Messiah, we have the picture of a small group of men and women who accepted him and followed him. It is sometimes suggested that Mark's portrayal of the disciples is so unsympathetic, and that he depicts them in such a harsh light, that he must have been gunning for them – or for those whom they represent. Is he perhaps attacking the church leaders of his day? Or is he using the Twelve as symbolic figures, in order to remind the Christians in his community that the path of discipleship was by no means obvious or easy?

The theme of discipleship is introduced at the very beginning of the Gospel. After the prologue and the opening summary in 1.14–15, we are told of the call of Simon and Andrew, James and John. Soon after, we have the call of Levi. In every case, these men respond immediately to the summons; they down tools with the alacrity which is allegedly shown today by workers hearing the shop steward's whistle. They abandon their means of employment in order to follow Jesus – a fact of which Peter reminds Jesus later in the Gospel. These scenes impress us in two ways: on the one hand, we see the authority of Jesus, who calls men to follow him and is instantly obeyed. On the other, we are reminded of the total demands that his call to discipleship makes.

In Mark 3.6 we have a turning-point in the story. The Pharisees and Herodians plot together to kill Jesus; the religious and political authorities have now come out against Jesus; already they have rejected his message. Jesus then withdraws with his disciples to the lakeside, and appoints twelve of them – first of all to be with him, and secondly to be sent out to preach and cast out demons. The three central characters in the group, Simon, James and John, are all given new names – signs of their new identity. The appointment of twelve, chosen from a larger group, suggests that they are to be the nucleus of Israel. In contrast to those who might have been expected to be the representatives of Israel, but who have chosen to oppose Jesus, these twelve are to form the group which is found in company with the Messiah, and to whom he delegates his own authority. The story which follows underlines the division that is taking place. It is in fact two stories, which Mark has woven together in his typical manner. Jesus' friends or family – the Greek is imprecise, but in view of the ending of the story it is more likely that the latter is meant – try to put a stop to Jesus' activities, because they think that he is out of his mind. At the same time, scribes come down from Jerusalem to see what is going on – men with more authority than the local officials we have met so far – and pronounce that Jesus is possessed by Beelzebul. Jesus denounces their blasphemy; they are attributing to Satan what is in fact the work of the Holy Spirit; their hard-heartedness is incorrigible, their sin unforgivable. But if Jesus denounces the official representatives of Judaism, he also disowns the members of his own family. When they arrive, they stand outside. And they remain outside, calling for Jesus to come to them. They do not belong to the company of Jesus' followers. 'Who are my mother and brothers?' asks Jesus, when he receives their message. In order to belong to his family, one must belong to his company; one must join the group of disciples, not stand outside. It is those who have responded to the message of Jesus, who accept his call to do the will of God, who belong to his company.

From this time onwards, the disciples are almost always in Jesus' company. Back in chapter 1, Jesus rose early in the morning and went away alone to pray; the disciples had to come chasing after him. But now he has appointed them to be with him – and with him they are. Even when Jesus sends them out on a mission in 6.12, we are told nothing about what he did until their return. So in Mark 4.10, when Jesus is 'alone', the disciples are there too. From now on, this group is contrasted with the crowd, instead of with Jewish officials or Jesus' family. To the crowd, who are outside (like Jesus' mother and brothers), everything remains in parables. It is there for them to understand, and they ought to understand – just as the scribes from Jerusalem ought to have understood. The disciples understand, because they join the group of Jesus' followers – and it is not only the Twelve who are so privileged, but 'those who are about him with the Twelve' as well. To the disciples, Jesus explained everything (vv. 33f.).

Nevertheless, the disciples are somewhat slow in the uptake. 'Don't you understand this parable?' asks Jesus in 4.13. 'How will you understand any of them?' They fare little better with the miracles. At the end of chapter 4 we have the first of a series of miracles – the stilling of the storm. 'Why are you afraid?' asks Jesus. 'Have you no faith?' Do they not realize who he is? But they don't – at least not fully, though they do get as far as putting the right question: 'Who is this,' they ask, 'that even wind and sea obey him?'

In chapter 6, Jesus sends the Twelve out to preach and heal; their mission to a wider area contrasts with the story in vv. 1–6, where Jesus teaches in the synagogue in his own town, and is met by disbelief. Jesus warns his disciples that they, too, may meet a hostile reception; if so, they are to shake the dust from their shoes when they leave. It was the symbolic action made by Jews leaving Gentile territory, and suggests that those who refuse to receive Jesus' messengers are no longer regarded as members of Israel.

Later in this chapter we have the story about the one occasion when Jesus leaves all his disciples. He goes to pray, and sends them across the lake. But without him, they are soon in trouble, and he has to come to their aid. But when they see him they are terrified, for they do not realize who he is. They have not understood about the loaves, comments Mark, because their hearts were hardened.

Perhaps this is why Jesus repeats the miracle of the loaves in chapter 8. It is sometimes suggested that Mark has incorporated two already-existing cycles of tradition, each of which included a feeding miracle and a crossing of the lake, the first ending in the healing of a deaf mute and the second in the cure of a blind man. But the stories of the two crossings are very different – except that in each the disciples are rebuked for their failure to understand the miracles of the loaves – and the first cycle contains extra material not in the second. Moreover, although there are similarities between the two healing narratives, and Mark clearly sees a parallel between blindness and deafness, the two stories are not the same. It seems much more probable that Mark has deliberately built up the sequence of stories, in order to make his point. Presumably he has inherited two different traditions of a feeding miracle; he sees them as separate incidents, but recognizes that they are almost identical. Why, Mark must have wondered, did Jesus feed the people twice? As we have already seen, there is no evidence for the popular explanation that Mark thought that the participants on one occasion were Jewish, and Gentile on the other. Mark provides us with his own explanation in 8.14–21. Jesus repeated the miracle because the disciples did not understand it the first time. On this second occasion, Jesus gives them some private tuition in the boat. Presumably the penny drops, since at Caesarea Philippi Peter is able to respond to the question put to them directly by Jesus about his own identity.

The clue to what is happening is provided by Mark in the

stories which immediately precede and follow the somewhat enigmatic conversation between Jesus and his disciples in the boat. The Pharisees come to Jesus and demand a sign. Jesus refuses; no sign will be given to this generation. The demand of the Pharisees is extraordinary, following as it does on the second feeding miracle. It is interesting to discover that the Johannine version of the story contains precisely the same phenomenon. In John 6.30, the Jews ask Jesus what sign he does, so that they may see and believe in him. Although they have eaten their fill of the loaves, nevertheless they have failed to see the signs that Jesus does (v. 26). In both Mark and John, we have people seeing the signs that Jesus did, and failing to recognize them as such. So they come to Jesus and demand another! But Jesus refuses to perform signs in order to persuade them; the signs are already there, waiting to be seen by those who have eyes. The disciples are in danger of the same disease as the Pharisees; their hearts, too, are somewhat hardened. 'Do you not yet understand?' asks Jesus. The answer is 'Yes – in part', for the story that follows is of the blind man whose eyes are opened in stages. It was, I think, R. H. Lightfoot who first pointed out the parallel between the story of the blind man and Caesarea Philippi, and suggested that the disciples' eyes were finally opened to the truth.[1] But Lightfoot seems to have been somewhat over-optimistic in his assessment of the disciples' comprehension! For Mark depicts them as only half understanding throughout the rest of his Gospel. From beginning to end the disciples are like the man who appears in 9.24, believing and not believing. They act as a foil, in turn, to outsiders of all kinds on the one hand – crowd, family, leaders of Israel, the nation, all of whom have hardened hearts – and Jesus himself on the other, who is the only person who sees clearly the significance of what is taking place.

But we are only just beginning with the theme of discipleship. The next section of the Gospel, from 8.27 to 10.45, contains all the predictions of Jesus' passion and resurrection, given in private to the disciples; but it contains also a great deal of teaching on the meaning of discipleship. One recent study of these chapters suggests that it is deliberately cast in the form of a journey from Caesarea Philippi to Jerusalem – from the acknowledgment of Jesus as Messiah to the story of the cross.[2] The disciples are the ones who accompany Jesus on that journey. And just as the section is introduced by a story about a blind man who gains his sight, so it ends in the same way, with a story about another blind man whose sight is restored – Bartimaeus, who hails Jesus as he reaches the end of his journey.

The meaning of discipleship is spelt out clearly at the very beginning of the section. Those who wish to be Jesus' disciples must deny themselves, take up a cross, and follow him. In a twentieth-century setting, the words have lost their bite. Self-denial is not ascetism, nor the denial of certain pleasures; rather, 'It is the opposite of self-affirmation, of putting value on one's being, one's life, one's position before man or God, of claiming rights and privileges . . .'[3] To take up the cross was a vivid – and spine-chilling – image to men and women of the first century, especially for the population of Galilee and for the slaves of the Roman empire, from whom many Christians were drawn. Did Mark take the call literally? Luke has toned it down, adding the phrase 'daily'; but one can be executed only once! Perhaps Mark felt that the disciples had failed Jesus precisely because, at the end, they were not prepared to be crucified with him. For Christians of his own day, such a fate might not be the inevitable consequence of following Jesus, but the disciple must be prepared even for that: and those who truly denied themselves – who put no value on themselves, and made no claims for themselves – would be ready to take up the cross and follow Jesus. Commentators frequently shy away from suggestions that discipleship is seen in terms of the imitation of Christ in the New Testament, but there is no doubt that

Mark sees it in these terms in the chapters that follow.

The challenge of Jesus to men to follow him is issued to the crowds as well as to the disciples. Mark does not tell us what they made of it. In fact, the challenge makes no sense unless it is heard in the context of the teaching which immediately precedes it about the suffering of the Son of man – teaching which, according to Mark, is addressed to disciples alone. Once again, we have an idea which cannot be grasped by outsiders, and which needs to be spelt out to disciples, as the rebuke by Jesus of Peter in the preceding verse demonstrates. But the challenge is issued to all; it is up to those who hear it to respond. And for those who accept the challenge, there is reward. Just as the Son of man will be vindicated after suffering by being raised from the dead (v. 31), so those who are prepared to follow Jesus and to lose their lives for his sake may expect to find life. But those who refuse his challenge will find that the Son of man does not acknowledge them as members of his community when he himself is vindicated.

In the next story, which is the account of the transfiguration, Jesus is accompanied by only three of his disciples – Peter, James and John. They alone had witnessed the raising of Jairus' daughter, and they alone now witness the transfiguration of Jesus, which can be understood only when he has been raised from the dead (9.9). Does Mark think of these three as being closer to understanding than the others? If so, why? Or is it simply that the tradition he inherited continually singled out these three names? Certainly Peter does not give much sign of understanding what is happening. His proposal to erect booths suggests that the End has come, and that Elijah and Moses have come to stay; he has forgotten already that suffering must precede the glory. Moreover, he puts Jesus on a par with Moses and Elijah. But they vanish, and the voice from heaven picks out Jesus as one far greater than his predecessors. The disciples are commanded to hear him, and going down the mountain they attempt to do so, though they cannot understand his words about resurrection.

Meanwhile, the rest of the disciples, left on their own without Jesus, are doing badly, having failed to heal an epileptic boy. Jesus' rebuke puts them on a par with the Pharisees: 'O faithless generation – how long must I put up with you?' At the end of the story, however, they are told that what they needed to perform the cure was prayer. The comment about lack of faith seems to belong to another strand in the story, which centres on the child's father rather than the disciples. The repetitiveness of the narrative suggests that in fact two stories have been woven together. For Mark, the father is a symbol of discipleship, like the blind man in chapter 8: he believes – yet he only half believes. His confession of faith, 'I believe', is immediately followed by his appeal for help, 'Help my unbelief'. He needs help to believe that his child can be healed. The description of the healing suggests that we are meant to see that as a symbol of a more fundamental belief. For in being healed, the child is left looking like a corpse, and he has to be raised up. Mark's language (Jesus 'lifted him up, and he arose') points us forward to the resurrection.

And immediately (to steal Mark's own favourite phrase) we return to the theme of what is to happen to the Son of man, and of the death and resurrection that await him. But the disciples cannot understand the teaching and were afraid to ask. As though to demonstrate their failure to understand, Mark tells us of their dispute on the way about greatness. Those who follow Jesus on the way certainly should not be quarrelling about greatness! They are apparently no nearer understanding Jesus' words about death and resurrection than they were at the end of chapter 8. So Jesus spells out once again what discipleship means, in the same kind of paradoxical language as before. Last time it was put in terms of life and death; this time it is put in terms of greatness and humility. Jesus spells out the lesson by taking a child in his arms and telling them that whoever receives a child like this in his name receives him. Now one of the unsolved problems in Mark is the strange fact that Mark seems to have muddled up two sayings about children. If we look at the story of the disciples rebuffing children in 10.13–16 we find that it leads into a saying about receiving the kingdom of God like a child. The odd thing is that the saying in 9.37 would fit much better into the second story, at 10.15, and *vice versa.* One possibility is that the two stories have got muddled up and the sayings transposed. Matthew seems to agree, since in his version of the story told in Mark 9 he has a parallel to the saying in Mark 10.15, and when he comes to the second story, he omits the saying altogether.[4] If there was a mix-up, when did it take place? Perhaps at the stage of oral tradition. Perhaps the two sayings about children were originally separate, not belonging to either story. Or could it have been a mistake on Mark's part? Was it perhaps a deliberate 'mistake'? If we take this story in Mark 9.33–37 on its own, then I think we must say that the saying in 10.15 about the need to be like a child might form a better conclusion. But in the context in which Mark has set it, perhaps we can begin to understand his logic. The disciples quarrel about which of them is greatest. But instead of worrying about their own position they should be concerned for the weakest and most humble member of the community; and in receiving the one who is weak and humble, they will be receiving Jesus himself. Once again, the disciples are pointed firmly to Jesus' own example.

The next story is about the exorcist who casts out demons in Jesus' name. The disciples have forbidden him, since he is not of their company; they are concerned for their own status and privileges. The story seems to reflect uneasiness in the Christian community about who did and who did not belong to their number. Like the sayings that follow, its theme is that of the importance of attitudes to fellow Christians.

Chapter 10 begins with a question from the Pharisees, and we are back to a familiar pattern; Jesus gives an answer, and then has to spell it out again to the disciples in private. There follows the story in which the disciples rebuff children and are in turn rebuked. Once again, they are demonstrating their lack of understanding; this time Jesus is indignant. In rebuffing children, the disciples are rebuffing those to whom the kingdom of God belongs – and showing how far they themselves are from entering that kingdom. Once again, a saying which does not seem to be the right ending for the story taken in isolation turns out to fit it very well in the Markan context.

The story of the man who comes to ask Jesus how to inherit eternal life is the story of a good man – a pious Jew who keeps the commandments and wishes to serve God – who lacks one thing: he refuses the call of Jesus to follow him. In 8.34 the call was to deny self, take up the cross and follow; this time it is to sell all he has, give it to the poor, and follow. But the demand is too great. The man's story is a foil to that of the disciples; they have left everything in order to follow Jesus. And they are promised reward: in following Jesus they will be saved, and will enter the kingdom of God.

And so we come to the third great prediction of Jesus' death and resurrection. Jesus walks ahead of his disciples; they follow him, but they are afraid (10.33). Their amazement shows that they do not really understand – and so does the incident that follows, when James and John demand the best seats in the kingdom. This time Jesus spells out clearly the link between his own suffering and theirs. Those who want to share his glory must share his cup and baptism. Those who are called to be rulers in the Christian community must follow the example of their master – who is master through being a servant, and who gives his life for his people. Once again, we have the theme of discipleship as the imitation of Christ, though here it is linked with the idea that his death and resurrection are in some unique way 'for' them.

The end of the journey brings us to the road outside Jericho: the story of Bartimaeus, the blind man who has at least a glimmering of understanding, and who, when his sight is restored, follows Jesus 'in the way' – the way that leads into Jerusalem, and to the cross.

This is the end of the great section on the meaning of discipleship, but of course the disciples do not disappear from the story at this point. We have already looked at some of the incidents in Jerusalem, many of which show the confrontation between Jesus and the religious authorities. But in chapter 13 we have another section of teaching given in private to the disciples – or rather to the four disciples, who have been with Jesus from the beginning, for Andrew is included this time, with Peter and James and John. The important verses for our theme are vv. 9–13, which refer specifically to the sufferings which Jesus' disciples may expect – to persecution for his sake. Immediately before his own passion and death, Jesus spells out what following him means – and the predictions 'echo' his own story: 'They will deliver you up to councils; you will be beaten in synagogues; you will stand before governors and kings to bear testimony to them. You will be brought to trial. Brother will deliver up brother to death. You will be hated by all for my name's sake.'[5] The disciples are still being called on to deny themselves, to take up a cross, and follow Jesus. Although they fail to do so when Jesus is arrested, the opportunity to do so will come again.

Ostensibly, Jesus' words in chapter 13 are a prophecy of the destruction of the temple. In fact, they are more in the nature of a warning to the disciples. They may find themselves caught up in the sufferings which are going to come on the nation. Certainly they will be involved in suffering as disciples. But they are not to be dismayed. What *they* must do is to preach the gospel (v. 10), to stand firm (v. 13) and watch. This last theme is spelt out in the parable of the man on a journey at the end of the chapter. His servants do not know at what time of the night he will arrive; therefore they must be ready and watch.

The command to watch is the final word in this chapter – the last command of Jesus before the passion narrative proper begins in chapter 14. It is echoed in Gethsemane, when Jesus again says to three of these four disciples – 'Watch!' (v. 34). But they cannot watch – they fall asleep. There are other echoes of this last paragraph of chapter 13 in the passion narrative; are they deliberate? The four watches of the night are evening, midnight, cockcrow and morning. In the evening, says Mark, Jesus held a supper with the disciples (14.17); at cockcrow, Peter denied him (14.68); in the morning, Jesus is taken before Pilate (15.1); it must be about midnight – though this is something that Mark does *not* take up – that Jesus prays in Gethsemane and is arrested, while the disciples fail to keep watch. This time they fail him; they fall asleep, they run away, they deny that they are his disciples. But chapter 13 suggests that they are to be given a second chance; and next time they must not fail.

Mark's emphasis on the cross is matched by his insistence that Christians must be prepared to share Jesus' suffering. Why? We are back with the problem raised in the last chapter. Was it to encourage those who were facing persecution, as has so often been supposed? At this point we can really only guess, but my hunch is that it is more likely that Mark wished to remind the Christians in his community that they must be prepared to expect persecution and suffering. The insistent reminders of the cost of discipleship suggest that at the moment their Christian commitment was not costing them particularly dear. Now if this was the situation, it might perhaps have gone hand in hand with a playing down of the sufferings of Jesus. But it is also possible that the opposite was true and that the members of Mark's church were simply failing to draw a link between Jesus' sufferings and the implications for their own lives. Certainly at a later stage in church history this became a great danger; for when the church becomes respectable, and being a Christian is no longer the automatic passport to ridicule and persecution, then we cease to identify ourselves with those disciples – or we reinterpret Jesus' demands to mean something far less demanding – and the shame and suffering are concentrated on to Jesus.

There is always a danger in stressing any theological truth, because truth has many facets; there is a danger in stressing the unique role of Jesus in dying for us, for it *can* mean that we forget the complementary truth that he is our example, that discipleship means following him and suffering with him. Is this what had happened in Mark's community? Certainly the temptation to by-pass the cross appears very clearly in his Gospel. Certainly something very similar seems to have happened in Corinth. Paul's scathing comments about the Corinthians suggests that they have grasped only half his message: they have understood the bit about Christ suffering, and the fact that this brings them life and joy and power and glory; but they see Christ, not as an example, but simply as a substitute. Paul has to spell out for them that the life of a Christian means conformity to the pattern of Christ. They do not want to take up a cross and march to the gallows, and they have failed to grasp the paradox of the cross, which demands that men and women must be identified with the shame and the suffering in order to share the life and glory which come through the cross.

Is this what Mark's readers have forgotten? I do not know – but certainly it is something that Mark himself never forgets. Suffering is as inevitable for the disciple as it is for Jesus; the cross is the mark of the Christian. He offers no explanation of why it is necessary. This is the way that Jesus went, and it is the way that his disciples must go also. True, in the Gospel, they cut a sorry figure. Yet, in the end they will follow him. You *will* drink my cup, says Jesus. You will be handed over for my sake. You will *not* be ashamed of me.

And so we come to the end – and what an extraordinary end it is. Mark seems to abandon us in the middle of the story. We feel let down, left in mid-air, hovering on the edge of Easter, with nothing in the way of evidence except a few women's tale of an empty tomb. We expect more than this. Clearly others have felt the same way. Two editors have had attempts at rounding Mark's story off.[6] The other three evangelists all completed their Gospels with stories of the risen Christ. It is only Mark who abandons us at dawn on Easter morning.

But did he abandon us? Many have found it hard to believe that he did. They have supposed either that Mark wrote more – and that the end of the Gospel was lost. Or that he planned to write more, and was prevented from doing so. Prevented by what? Perhaps death overtook the disciple who saw so clearly the need to be prepared to die for his faith. But if Mark did write more, and the end of his Gospel was lost, it is hard to explain how that happened – or why it was not replaced. More and more students of the Gospel have become convinced that Mark in fact deliberately ended his book at 16.8; there is no more because he did not write more, and he did not intend to write more. If the Gospel seems unfinished to us, that is because we are used to the other Gospels and expect Mark to do things in the same way. But the different evangelists tend to do all sorts of things differently, and their endings are no exception. Matthew ends his Gospel with the command of Jesus to his disciples to go into the whole world and preach the gospel; he presents Jesus throughout his Gospel as the one who instructs the disciples and it is no surprise that the final story is another instruction – an instruction to teach. Luke ends his Gospel with the disciples in Jerusalem, worshipping in the temple – again a common feature in Luke. John ends with the declaration that what is written is meant to bring his readers to faith – a typically Johannine sentiment. And Mark, if he indeed meant to end at 16.8, shocked the grammarians by ending with the word 'for' – but then, grammarians are shocked all the way through by Mark's Greek. Even odder, however, he ends with the extraordinary statement: they were afraid.

But this, too, is typical of Mark. For all through his Gospel fear, awe, amazement have been the typical human reaction to divine action seen in Jesus. People have been afraid because they have not understood; it is not surprising if the women, confronted with the most stupendous divine act, react in the same way. And how extraordinary that Mark should end with a story about women! In Mark's Gospel, these women are the connecting link between Jesus' death and burial and his resurrection. After the disciples' flight, they alone watch his death and note his place of burial. And they are the only witnesses of the resurrection – or rather, of the report of the resurrection. And what use, a Jew must have asked, is a second-hand report by women? One needed two male witnesses to establish the truth of anything; why should one give any credence to the report of women? If Mark *did* intend to end his Gospel at 16.8, then he certainly did not try to persuade his readers by offering them anything in the nature of cast-iron evidence. All we have is a second-hand message, sent to the disciples by a few women, who were too scared to pass it on. And how typical of the Markan Jesus that message is: 'Go and you will see him.' Not 'You will see him, and then you must go.' The message *demands* a response. 'Stretch out your hand,' says Jesus to the man with a shrivelled hand. How *can* he stretch out a hand which is shrivelled? But he does. 'Stand up and walk' to a paralyzed man. How can a paralytic get up? But he does. 'Go', runs the message to the disciples – to men paralyzed with fear; it is only as they go that they will see him.

As Mark leaves it, his narrative stresses two things. First,

Jesus has risen. Second, he has gone ahead into Galilee. The women are invited to see the empty tomb; the disciples are promised that they will see Jesus. The message picks up the saying in 14.28, where Jesus tells the disciples that after his resurrection he will go before them into Galilee. The verb used in both passages, *pro-agō*, means 'to go before' and in chapter 14 it seems to have the sense of 'to lead', for the context speaks about the shepherd and his sheep. Here in 16.7 we perhaps need to understand it in the sense of 'precede', for Jesus has gone ahead of the disciples. Jesus goes before his disciples, but they have failed to keep up with him; now he summons them back. He is still their leader, and still acknowledges them as his disciples, in spite of their disloyalty and denial. They have been ashamed of him – but he is still prepared to own them. Peter denied knowing Jesus, but the shepherd knows his sheep and leads them still. The remarkable thing about this scene is that in spite of their abysmal failure, they are still disciples – even Peter is invited. And the invitation is to begin again. Is this why they are summoned to Galilee? Various explanations have been given for the reference to Galilee; it has been suggested that this will be the place of the parousia; or that it is the place for mission to the Gentiles. But Mark gives no hint of either idea. In his story, Galilee was the place where Jesus called the disciples, trained them, taught them and sent them out. If Jesus calls them now to follow him to Galilee, is it not because he is gathering his scattered sheep, calling each one of them once again to deny self, take up the cross, and follow him? His words are words of forgiveness, for those who have failed and disowned him.

'Go and tell his disciples', says the messenger to the women. They obey the first part of his command – the command to go; they rush out at full speed. But they say nothing to anyone! Confronted with the mighty action of God, they are overcome by trembling and astonishment. Mark's last words describe human failure – human inability to grasp the reality of what was happening. The moment has come to speak, but they are struck dumb. Up to this point in the narrative, the women have been the one group to escape rebuke. While everyone else seemed to have hard hearts and closed minds, the few women who appeared in the narrative were commended for their faith. They alone stood by Jesus at his death. But now, confronted with this act, even they cannot take it in.

If we don't like Mark's ending, and think he cannot really have intended to end there, then perhaps it is because we are looking for the wrong thing. What we expect to find at the end of the Gospel is the knock-down proof, the evidence that proves that Jesus has indeed been raised from the dead, that he is the Messiah, the Son of God. But as with every other story in the Gospel, the evidence is there for those who have eyes to see it. It is there – but in order to see it, it is necessary to believe – to be a disciple. 'Go, and you will see him,' says the messenger to the disciples. And this is the message of Mark to his readers. Is it not, after all, a good place to end the Gospel? For this is the real beginning of discipleship; and it is the beginning for Mark's own readers, who do not 'see' Jesus in any physical way. The promise is to them, as well as to the eleven frightened disciples. Follow Jesus; that is the only way in which you will find him.

Notes

Chapter One

1. The tradition was recorded by Papias, Bishop of Hierapolis, writing about AD 140, who says that he learned it from 'the Elder'. It is known to us through the work of Eusebius, a church historian of the fourth century, who quotes from Papias' writings.

2. Authors as different and as far apart chronologically as E. Renan (*Vie de Jésus*, 1863), Charles Gore (*Jesus of Nazareth*, 1929) and C. H. Dodd (*The Founder of Christianity*, 1970), all use Mark's outline as their starting point.

3. *History and Interpretation in the Gospels*, London 1935, pp. 61ff.; *The Gospel Message of St Mark*, Oxford 1950, pp. 15ff.

4. The latest edition of the Greek text, the 26th edition of Nestle-Aland, published in 1979, leaves a gap after v. 13.

5. C. K. Barrett, *The Holy Spirit and the Gospel Tradition*, London 1947, p. 125, describes it as an 'attractive conjecture'.

6. Babylonian Talmud, Hagigah 15a.

7. Rom. 8.

8. 'Temptation' is perhaps not the best English word to use in this context, even though it is the traditional one. 'Testing' is a better translation.

Chapter Two

1. 'The Framework of the Gospel Narrative', *Expository Times* 43, 1932, pp. 396–400, reprinted in C. H. Dodd, *New Testament Studies*, Manchester 1953, pp. 1–11.

2. The outline given by Dodd consists of the 'summaries' of Jesus' activity which occur from time to time in the course of the narrative. K. L. Schmidt, whose work Dodd was attacking, had argued that they were the work of the evangelist himself, composed to link the various units of tradition together. Dodd argued, on the contrary, that they were part of the tradition, and that Mark had split up what had once been a continuous narrative. The outline, as Dodd reconstructs it, consists of Mark 1.14–15, 21–22, 39; 2.13; 3.7b–19; 4.33–34; 6.7, 12–13, 30.

He suggests that it falls into three stages: 'A. Synagogue preaching and exorcism in Capernaum and elsewhere; B. Teaching, healing, and exorcism by the seashore, in the presence of vast crowds from all Palestine and beyond; C. Retirement in the Hill-country with a small circle of disciples, who are sent on preaching and healing tours' (op. cit., p. 8). It will be noted that though Dodd speaks of an outline of the whole of Jesus' ministry, the one that he offers covers only the Galilaean ministry.

3. 'The Order of Events in St Mark's Gospel – an examination of Dr Dodd's Hypothesis', in *Studies in the Gospels, Essays in memory of R. H. Lightfoot*, edited by D. E. Nineham, Oxford 1957, pp. 223–39.

4. *A Study in St Mark*, London 1951; *St Matthew and St Mark*, London 1966.

5. *The Evangelists' Calendar*, London 1978.

6. C. E. B. Cranfield, *The Gospel according to Saint Mark*, Cambridge Greek Testament Commentary, rev. edn 1972, p. 66.

7. *The Parables of the Kingdom*, London 1935.

8. J. Jeremias, *The Parables of Jesus*, revd edn, London 1963, pp. 247f., lists 6 parables in Mark, 23 in Matthew, and 29 in Luke.

9. The verb 'to teach' is used of Jesus fifteen times in Mark; on ten occasions he is addressed as 'Teacher' by his disciples or by others, and on two more he is referred to by that title.

Chapter Three

1. There are two ways of punctuating v. 28: the phrase 'with authority' can be taken either with the preceding phrase, or with the words that follow. In the former case, the authority is linked with the new teaching which the crowd is hearing, and their comment echoes the statement made in v. 22; in the latter, the authority is linked with the exorcism, and Jesus is said to command the unclean spirits with authority. Whichever punctuation we choose, however, the result is the same; for if it is the teaching which is 'with authority', then the power over demons is apparently dependent on that authoritative teaching, and if it is the exorcism, then we have two parallel statements about the authority of Jesus in teaching and healing. In either case, Mark has welded teaching and exorcism together, and the authority of Jesus is seen in both. This close connection between speech and action is not surprising when we remember that in first century Jewish thought word and action were not so widely separated as they are for us today.

2. 1.32–34; 3.10–12.

3. The more familiar form of the name, Beelzebub, meaning 'Lord of the flies', seems to be the result of an early corruption; it is found in Latin and Syriac translations, but not in any of the Greek manuscripts.

4. Since the demoniac in chapter 5 was living in what may have been Gentile territory, it is possible that he, too, was thought to be a Gentile. But Mark makes no mention of this. Moreover, this man – or rather the demons speaking through him – confess Jesus to be the Holy One of God.
5. D. E. Nineham, *The Gospel of St Mark*, Harmondsworth 1963, p. 147.
6. Alan Richardson, *The Miracle Stories of the Gospels*, London 1941, p. 92.
7. Op. cit., pp. 97f.
8. Op. cit., p. 215.
9. Although Mark speaks about hearts being hardened (3.5; 6.52; 8.17), the phrase denotes failure to understand (the heart being the seat of comprehension), rather than what we should understand by 'hard-heartedness'.

Chapter Four

1. E.g. T. J. Weeden, *Mark: Traditions in Conflict*, Philadelphia 1971.
2. W. Wrede, *Das Messiasgeheimnis in den Evangelien*, Göttingen 1901, ET *The Messianic Secret*, Cambridge and London 1971. Wrede was, in his approach, a redaction critic years ahead of his time. In contrast to his contemporaries, who assumed that Mark was presenting an historical account of the life of Jesus, he recognized that Mark's concerns were primarily theological. Contrary to what is often said, Wrede did not suggest that Mark created the messianic secret. In fact, he dismissed that idea as impossible, and maintained that it must already have been embedded in the tradition that Mark used. Nevertheless, he believed that Mark had an important part in the way in which the theme is presented in his Gospel: the evangelist inherited the motif in the tradition, but used it in his own way. Whether Wrede was correct in maintaining that the idea originated in the tradition rather than in the life of Jesus is another matter; certainly his view that the life of Jesus was entirely unmessianic in character raises considerable problems.
3. In Matthew and Luke the reply is far less straightforward. Matthew has 'You have said so' (26.64), while Luke divides both question and answer into two, and has 'If I tell you, you will not believe . . . You say that I am' (22.67, 70). Because of the difficulty of explaining why the later evangelists should make the bold declaration in Mark more tentative, some commentators argue that he, too, originally wrote something like their 'You have said it', and a few texts do in fact read

this. But this variant is probably due to assimilation to Matthew's text.

4. This section confirms what I have already concluded about the scene at Caesarea Philippi: Jesus' command to silence cannot be explained as a rejection of the title 'Messiah'. There is an interesting parallel between the two scenes, since in both, immediately after the confession that he is the Messiah, Jesus begins to speak of himself as the Son of man.

Chapter Five

1. The 'Mahdi' is the religious leader expected by some Muslim sects. The term means 'guided', and has been applied to various Muslim teachers, as well as being used to express the future hope.

2. See G. Vermes, *Jesus the Jew*, London 1973, pp. 160–91; Maurice Casey, *Son of Man*, London 1979. The basic meaning of the phrase, in both Hebrew and Aramaic, is simply 'man'.

3. I have attempted to do so in 'Is the Son of Man problem really insoluble?', in *Text and Interpretation*, ed. E. Best and R. McL. Wilson, Cambridge 1979, pp. 155–68.

4. I have explored these parallels in *The Son of Man in Mark*, London 1967.

Chapter Six

1. J. A. T. Robinson, 'The Relation of the Prologue to the Gospel of St John', *New Testament Studies*, Vol. 9, 1963, pp. 120–9.

2. Mekilta on Exodus 16.33.

3. *Dialogue with Trypho* 8.4.

4. The evidence is set out by W. R. Telford, *The Barren Temple and the Withered Tree*, Sheffield 1980, pp. 132–204.

5. W. R. Telford, op. cit., pp. 95–127, suggests that the saying in Mark 11.23 refers to the removal of the temple mount in the last days; instead of being lifted up, as was expected, it is to be cast down.

Chapter Seven

1. T. J. Weeden, *Mark: Traditions in Conflict*, Philadelphia 1971.

2. M. D. Hooker, *Jesus and the Servant*, London 1959, pp. 74–9.

3. J. M. Creed, *The Gospel according to St Luke*, London 1930, p. lxxii.

4. Gospel of Thomas 65–6.

Chapter Eight

1. *History and Interpretation in the Gospels*, London 1935, pp. 90f.
2. Ernest Best, *Following Jesus*, Sheffield 1980.
3. Ibid, p. 37.
4. Matt. 18.1–5; 19.13–15.
5. The link between ch. 13 and the passion narrative was pointed out by R. H. Lightfoot, *The Gospel Message of St. Mark*, Oxford 1950, pp. 48–59.
6. The language and style of the passage included in our English Bibles as vv. 9–20 is quite different in language and style from the rest of Mark, and is missing from some of the best Greek mss. The alternative, shorter ending, is included by a few mss. before vv. 9–20, and is clearly another attempt to complete the story.

Index of Modern Authors

References in the text are listed according to the page numbers; those occurring in the notes (pp. 125–9) are listed by the numbers of the chapter (roman numeral) and the note (arabic).

Index of Subjects

Index of Biblical References

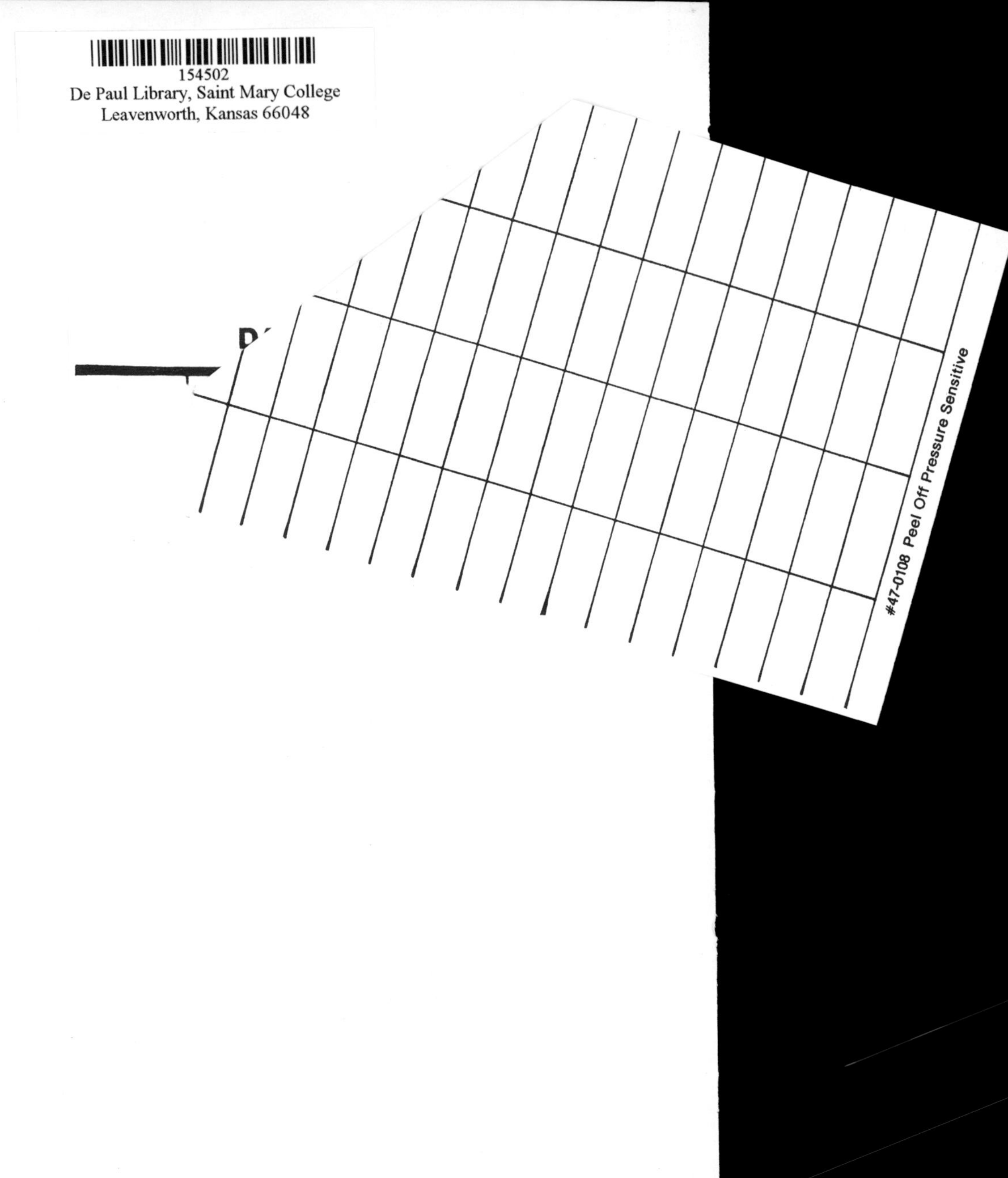
#47-0108 Peel Off Pressure Sensitive